BOOKS BY AUTHOR DON JANS

MY GRANDCHILDREN'S AMERICA WILL IT STILL BE THE LAND OF THE FREE AND THE HOME OF THE BRAVE

GOODBYE CONSTITUTION, FREEDOM, AMERICA

THE ROAD TO TYRANNY INDIVIDUALISM TO COLLECTIVISTM

TWO VISIONS OF AMERICA

1

TWO
VISIONS
OF
AMERICA

TWO

VISIONS

OF

AMERICA

DON JANS

COVER BY LINDA YAUSSI

ISBN   978-0-578-55148-7

COPYWRGHT – PENDING   2019

SMEA PUBLSHING

I AM DEDICATING "TW0 VISIONS OF AMERICA" TO THE MEMORY OF THE TWO PEOPLE WHO TAUGHT ME THE MOST AND MEANT EVERYTHING TO ME.

MY UNCLE MEL AND AUNT EILEEN

Uncle Mel was and is my hero. He taught me that a question is a better way of persuading than is an answer. Uncle Mel was the least pretentious person I knew. He was never interested in showing another how smart he was, but instead was more concerned with helping another person discover what he already knew.

Aunt Eileen was the kindest most loving person I knew. She taught me that to love is to love another person for themselves and not what we envision or want them to be. When Aunt Eileen talked about the wonderful accomplishments of others, she never used but if they had only done it my way it could have been even better.

I love and miss you Uncle Mel and Aunt Eileen. Rest in peace. Until we meet again.

Melvin Jans   9/6/1925   12/1/2017

Eileen Jans   2/24/1927 2/21/2016

PREFACE

"We must stand for true American values" is a common phrase uttered by those on both sides of the political spectrum. Those who support a cradle to grave welfare state, use this phrase. Those who believe the role of the government is to strive to provide conditions that enable prosperity with no government subsidies, use this phrase. Those who believe all our borders should be open to all who wish to enter with no expectations of assimilation, use this phrase. Those who believe we should impose strict criteria along with the expectation of assimilation when choosing those we allow to become a part of our society, use this phrase. We can draw contrasts in many different areas, and we learn that both sides of any topic will identify their position as the position that identifies with "true American values."

"True American values" has come to mean whatever the user wants it to mean. When something can mean anything, we want it to mean, then it has no meaning at all. This is what has happened to the meaning of "true American values;" it no longer has any meaning. We have become a "TWO VISIONS OF AMERICA." America is divided and there are two distinct visions of what America was and should become; of what "true American values" means. In America today, there are two totally different visions of the role government should have over society and over the lives of individual citizens. Throughout our history, Americans have had different philosophies on how we should arrive at a common goal. In America today, there are two different philosophies, but there is no longer a common goal. Each philosophy has its own goal, and the goals are polar opposites.

Some might describe this change as a revolution, but a study of American history would reveal this change to be evolutionary with a recent escalation. Even when the United States Constitution was drafted and ratified, different philosophies on the role government should have over all aspects of society and the individual existed. There was however a common goal, and that goal was to establish a functioning government that would maintain an international policy that would benefit the nation as a whole, as well as to have a functioning government that would maintain order and tranquility domestically but would not infringe on the natural rights of the individual; including but not limited to life, liberty, and property or as Jefferson said "the pursuit of happiness."

The different philosophies of the role government should play still exists, not only in our nation but in all societies. It is the end goal that has changed. Under one vision of America, the vision for government is to play the role of securing and promoting the United States internationally while assuring the preservation of our sovereignty. Domestically, it is the goal of that vision that the natural rights of each citizen, those rights granted by the Creator and not by man or government, are never infringed by man or government.

Under the other vision of America, the goal has changed. The vision of this philosophy emphasizes that internationally, the United States is not sovereign over its destiny, but must adhere to the dictates of an international order. This vision sees the United States as a part of the whole, and the goals and ambitions of the United States must fit within what is determined to be in the best interest of the whole as determined by global interests.

The same basic vision exists domestically. Domestically, this vision believes that natural rights of the citizen do not exist, but each citizen's rights are those government has determined is best for society as a whole. Life, liberty, and property or the pursuit of happiness, are now subjected to the dictates of government and granted by government to the individual subject to what government has determined is best for society.

The purpose of writing this book is not to pass judgement on one philosophy and vision over another. Instead, the purpose is to draw the contrast between the two. In drawing this contrast, it is necessary to review objectively the vision for our nation when it was founded. We must objectively review what the founders defined to be "true American values" and contrast those values with the two philosophies of today. We must objectively review the methods and tools implemented by the founders to maintain and enhance what they viewed as "true American values" and how those methods and tools were intended to operate. We must then contrast those methods and tools as implemented with how the two visions of today would have those methods and tools operate today.

It is the goal of this book, to assist each reader to determine for themselves what are "true American values." Once the reader has made their determination, it is the goal of the author to help the reader determine with which philosophy and vision they identify. We cannot exist as a unified nation if we are in fact a people with "TWO VISIONS OF AMERICA." We can have differences as to how we arrive at a specific goal, but the goal must be the same, just as our founders agreed on one goal. It is the hope of the author that "TWO VISIONS OF AMERICA" can help clarify the two visions and enable America to once again have a common goal. Even though we may differ on how to arrive at the goal, if we have a common goal, honest compromise can again be a part of our governing system.

This is a major undertaking. It is the result of the experience of having written "My Grandchildren's America," "Goodbye Constitution, Freedom, America," and "The Road to Tyranny," and the reaction to and feedback from those who have read one or more of the above. Just as those works were written for American citizens who are concerned about the direction, divisiveness, and internal condemnation of our nation, so too is "TWO VISIONS OF AMERICA." Although the author believes all can and will learn, the book is not written for academia or the self-proclaimed elite. This book is written, as were the others, for those who are concerned about the divide the United States faces and how we can again become a nation with differing philosophies, ideas, and visions, but with the common goal of America being that "shining city on the hill," showing the rest of the world the rewards of freedom and independence when we honor the idea that, "We are all created equal and are endowed by our creator with certain unalienable rights including the right to life, liberty, and the pursuit of happiness."

Although only one name appears as the author, projects of this nature are never the work of any one single contributor. The final product is a compilation of one, but with the assistance and input of many, contributing in many ways. I again want to thank my children for listening and acting interested in the numerous questions I asked them. Thank you for giving me honest feedback. Thank you, to a special lady Fern Pham, to my sister Deb and my brother-in-law Wayne, and to Cyndi Tingey for reading the raw transcript and giving me such valuable feedback. I also want to thank Pastor Greg Young. Beth Schoenberg, and Andrea Kaye for allowing me to go on their radio programs and air my thoughts on rights and entitlements. It was very helpful.

A special thanks to my granddaughters, Jadyn and Jillian, and Jadyn's friend Trinity Laiewski for being so patient with me while designing a cover. Sometimes grandfathers can be exasperating, but your patience and creativity are greatly appreciated.

A very special thanks goes to Linda Yaussi who took a hodgepodge of different drawings and ideas for the cover and brought it all together better than I had ever imagined.

TABLE OF CONTENTS

RIGHT OR ENTITLEMENT

The collectivist movement has confused mankind throughout the course of history by not making the proper delineation between a right or an entitlement. The collectivist movement within the United States, (and I specifically say the United States because that is our primary concern, but this is true of the universal collectivist movement) would have us believe that entitlements are rights. Consequently, we are told that health care is a right, that education is a right, that a basic income is a right, and that income and wealth equality are rights. We are further informed that these rights (entitlements) are mandated by the United States Constitution, and universally by the power of any government.

The concept of natural rights was discussed by people such as Thomas Aquinas, Thomas Hobbes, and John Locke. A distinguishing feature of natural rights or rights is that they are not granted by man or government, they are not enhanced by man or government, and they were always presented as to not be controlled by or limited by man or government. These rights, commonly referred to as life, liberty, and property, existed prior to government and were and should continue to be separate from the purview of government. An individual's natural right is not dependent upon another individual nor does one individual having a natural right take away anything from another. My right to liberty is totally independent of your right to liberty; the amount of liberty I have does not take away from your liberty.

Common definition of Natural Rights:

Natural rights are those rights that are not dependent on the laws or customs of any particular culture or government, and so are universal and inalienable (they cannot be repealed or restrained by human laws).

In contrast, an entitlement is based on the laws of man and is totally under the purview of government. For an individual to receive an entitlement, there must be another individual who sacrifices. Commonly this sacrifice is called a tax and is remitted to government, so the recipient can receive their entitlement. The rules for granting and confiscating required in this wealth sharing scheme, are determined by government. An individual can receive the entitlement only if another individual is penalized or taxed.

Definition of entitlement by the United States Senate:

entitlement - A Federal program or provision of law that requires payments to any person or unit of government that meets the eligibility criteria established by law. Entitlements constitute a binding obligation on the part of the Federal Government, and eligible recipients have legal recourse if the obligation is not fulfilled. Social Security and veterans' compensation and pensions are examples of entitlement programs.

When we are told for example that health care is a right, this is a lie and we are intentionally being deceived by the collectivist. History has shown that collectivists want entitlements to be perceived as rights by the general population so those receiving will become dependent upon the collectivist and those contributing will be shamed into believing their exercise of their natural rights are greedy and taking from another. The collectivist has used this deceit to gain power and control over the masses to enhance their power and life of luxury for centuries.

A society that cherishes freedom for all, protects and defends natural rights while limiting or eliminating government entitlements. This same society establishes a "safety net system" and "welfare system" that is the product of the natural goodness and charitable attitudes of, and under the control of the people of that free society. A society that adheres to the concept of limited government will remain a free and prosperous nation with a high standard of living for all and a very low percentage of the population considered to be living in poverty.

A society that strives for a society dominated by government entitlements, must take from the innovator and job creator to redistribute to the general public under the guise that these entitlements are rights. This has very often been referred to as "Hope and Change." What history has proven is that the promise of "Hope and Change" has always ended with an enslaved population that has willingly become servants to a tyrannical few who now control and limit the entitlements of the servants. These tyrannical few also believe natural rights are under their purview and come to control life, liberty, and property of all. This course always ends with the general population living in an equal status of poverty.

As you listen to the promises being made by the many collectivists in the United States today, remember that an entitlement is not a right but is a means to control and enslave all but the tyrannical few. When the tyrannical few have accomplished the enslavement of the masses, they will, based on history, also believe they are the grantor of natural rights, your right to life, liberty, and property.

FORMATION

"WHEN OUR FOUNDERS CREATED OUR GOVERNMENT, THEY UNDERSTOOD THAT THE GOVERNMENT THEY WERE CREATING, ANY GOVERNMENT THEY WOULD CREATE, IT WOULD BE THAT GOVERNMENT THAT WOULD BE THE SINGLE BIGGEST THREAT TO THE FREEDOMS THEY HAD JUST WON." Don Jans

Patrick Henry said, "The Constitution is not an instrument for the government to restrain the people. The Constitution is an instrument for the people to restrain the government, lest it (the government) should come to dominate our lives and thoughts."

THE UNITED STATES OF AMERICA IS UNIQUE. The American Revolution was unique. The formation of the United States as a nation, was unique. The basis on which the United States formed its government was unique. It is no longer politically correct, under one of "TWO VISIONS OF AMERICA," to state that the United States is an exceptional nation. Whether it is politically correct or not, the fact is the founding fathers, by forming the nation and government they did, changed the world. The United States is a unique nation and the way in which it changed the world makes the United States an exceptional nation.

The American Revolution was unique in many ways but here are five specific ways that contrast it with other revolutions.

1. In the American Revolution, the colonist leaders obeyed the will of the citizens, not vice versa.

The Declaration of Independence was also a Declaration of War. The American Colonists declared they would no longer be subjected to the tyranny of Great Britain, even though Great Britain was a very powerful nation, far superior in military might and economic resources than the colonies. Despite the odds against the American Colonists winning their freedom, the desire to be free from a tyrannical government prevailed. The American Revolution, unlike any other, changed all of history for the good. The American Revolution was the first in history to assert that ordinary people could tell their leaders what to do, and not the reverse.

2. The outcome of the American Revolution resulted in a stable Republic.

Our revolution immediately became the model for many other revolutions including the flawed French Revolution. Yet America's lasted and France's did not. The American Revolution resulted in the foundation of a stable and prosperous republic. Elsewhere, revolutions were followed by countless other revolutions, coups, and wars. The only form of revolution that followed the surrender of Cornwallis to Washington on October 19,1781 would have been repealing the Articles of Confederation and drafting and ratifying The Constitution of the United States of America.

3. Unlike other revolutions, the Revolutionary War never underwent an extremely violent phase, glutted with beheadings and torture of those who opposed or supported the revolution.

No time like the period of the Jacobin's occurred during or after the American Revolution. The American Revolution did not place somebody like Emperor Napoleon Bonaparte as the head of the government. A bloody civil war did not take place between two factions of American colonists like happened in Russia. A dictator, much like the

French Emperor emerged in Russia with Lenin and the Communist Party taking total control of the Russian people. The United States did have a civil war that took place about 80 years later.

4. "American Exceptionalism" was the origin for the Revolution.

Yes, the United States is unique, exceptional. American exceptionalism rests on four pillars that were found nowhere else; 1) a Protestant religious foundation; 2) the common law; 3) private property with written titles and deeds; and 4) a free market economy.

5. Unlike the initiators of other international revolutions, American colonies were truly threatened.

From their origin the American people had both a religious and a political philosophy of bottom-up governance. That explains why British attempts to regulate trade and introduce new taxes and laws that even potentially threatened to allow top-down control of the American colonies were viewed with sheer terror, viewed as tyrannical, and united the colonists immediately.

The values and integrity held by the American colonists differed from other revolutionaries in history. The American colonist's freedom was under attack from an outsider, and the colonists were fully determined to overcome this threat. The events of the war for independence and its results reveal the truth about the colonist's pursuit of justice and the honor involved in the colonists declaring their independence which was a declaration of war.

After the improbable victory of the American colonists over Great Britain, the colonists set about the onerous task of forming a nation. The distrust of government and the necessity to limit power and influence of government became the predominant factor in the formation of the new nation and new government the American colonist formed.

It is to be remembered that the general government is not to be charged with the whole power of making and administering laws. Its jurisdiction is limited to certain enumerated objects. James Madison **said in Federalist #14.**

The Founders distrusted strong governments. Their own experience and study of history taught them that overly powerful governments turned oppressive. But they also knew a government was necessary. In fact, they understood a stronger government than what they had at the beginning of our nation under the Articles of Confederation was necessary. By the time the Constitutional Convention convened in May of 1787, a consensus had developed that the Articles of Confederation were severely flawed, but there was uncertainty about what kind of government could sustain a republic through the ages. They knew it couldn't be too weak, but it also couldn't be too strong.

The Founders did not form a government and then hope for the best. Instead they designed an elaborate set of checks and balances so they could give the government enough power to govern, while harnessing it with multiple Lilliputian ropes that would hold it in place, so it didn't trample the people. From our high school civics class, we were taught about the checks and balances between the three branches, but teachers seldom mentioned the intended check of the national government by the states. Nor were we taught that the Founders wanted our national leaders selected and elected by different means as another check on a runaway government. Lastly, the Constitution ratified by the people was supposed to be the premier check to prevent our government from becoming oppressive.

Given the sometime contentious nature of the debate during the Constitutional Convention, perhaps it is prudent to move toward less contested and more factual terrain, where it is possible to better understand what the fuss was all about. What, in the end, did the Founding Fathers manage to do? Once both the inflated and judgmental rhetoric is brushed aside, what did they achieve?

At the most basic level, the Founders created the first modern nation-state based on principles demanding liberty. These principles include the democratic principle that political sovereignty in any government resides in the people and not in a divinely sanctioned monarchy as was the norm in the late 1700's; the capitalistic principle that economic productivity depends upon the release of individual energies in the marketplace rather than on state-sponsored policies; the moral principle that the individual, not the society or the state, is the sovereign unit in the political equation;

the judicial principle that all citizens are equal before the law; they established a modern nation state based on the principles of individualism and not collectivism. These principles are the political recipe for success, casting aside the European monarchies in the 18th and 19th centuries and the totalitarian regimes based on the ideology of collectivism of nations such as Germany, Japan, the Soviet Union, and members of the Soviet bloc in the 20th century.

The Founding Fathers defied conventional wisdom in four unprecedented achievements: first, they won a war for freedom and independence against the most powerful military and economic power in the world at the time; second, they established the first large-scale republic in the modern world; third, they founded political parties that institutionalized the concept of legitimate opposition but yet adhered to peaceful and orderly transfer of power; and fourth, they established the principle of the legal separation of church and state. Finally, all these achievements were won without the use of the guillotine, hangings, or the firing squad, which is to say without the violent purges that were a part of subsequent revolutions in places like France, Russia, and China. This was the overarching accomplishment that the British philosopher Alfred Lord North Whitehead had in mind when he stated that there were only two instances in the history of Western civilization when the political elite of an emerging empire behaved as well as one could reasonably expect: the first was Rome under Augustus, and the second was the United States under the Founding Fathers.

Thus far the identity, achievements, and failures of the Founding Fathers have been considered as if they were the expression of a composite personality with a singular orientation. But this would be wildly misleading. Founding Fathers is a plural noun, which means that the portrait of the American Revolution has many faces. To be sure, Washington was the first among equals, generally regarded, then and forever, as indispensable. But unlike revolutions that followed in France, Russia, China, and others where a single person came to embody the meaning of the revolutionary movement—Napoleon I, Vladimir Illich/Lenin, Joseph Stalin, Mao Zedong, Fidel Castro, Hugo Chávez – the revolutionary experience in the United States had multiple faces and multiple meanings that coexisted without ever devolving into a singular embodiment of authority. If one of the distinctive contributions of the American political tradition was a pluralistic conception of governance, its source was the multi-faceted character of the founding generation itself.

All the Founders agreed that American independence from Great Britain was nonnegotiable and that whatever government was established in lieu of British rule must be republican in character. Beyond this consensus, there was widespread disagreement, which surfaced most dramatically in the debate over ratification of the Constitution (1787–88). Two prominent Founders, Patrick Henry and George Mason, opposed ratification, because they believed, the Constitution created a central government that only replicated the arbitrary power of the British monarchy and Parliament. The divided politics of the 1790s further exposed the real differences within the founders. The Federalists, led by Washington, John Adams, and Hamilton, were opposed by the Republicans, led by Jefferson and James Madison. These factions disagreed over the proper allocation of federal and state power over domestic policy, the response to the French Revolution, the constitutionality of the Bank of the United States, and the core values of

American foreign policy. These differences often resulted in inflammatory rhetoric because nothing less than the "true meaning" of the American Revolution seemed at stake.

The ideological and contentious differences between the founders gave the American founding a distinctly argumentative tone that said all convictions, no matter how cherished, were still subjected to scrutiny. Much like the principle of checks and balances in the Constitution, the elevation of reasoned and rational argument created a permanent forum that generated a dynamic version of political stability.

When the founders signed the Declaration of Independence, the United States of America, in declaring their independence, adopted "the Laws of Nature and of Nature's God," proclaiming that men are "endowed by their Creator" with unalienable rights, appealed to "the Supreme Judge of the world," and concluded by expressing their reliance on "Divine Providence."

Nobody can doubt that those delegates in Philadelphia who adopted the Declaration of Independence believed in, and, based the nation's independence on, the Natural Law; that is, that God, in creating the universe, implanted in the nature of man a body of Law to which all human beings are subject, which is superior to all manmade law, and which is knowable by human reason as described by John Locke.

Eleven years later, another group of delegates, this time as representatives of the different States, met again in Philadelphia. This time the onerous task before them was to create a new structure of government for the United States, one that would establish "a more perfect union." They argued, they comprised, and in 1787 wrote the document that, was ratified by the several States; and became the law of the land in 1789 as the Constitution of the United States of America.

The Constitution was designed to be a practical document that would be the final authority for the operation of a more effective government. We do not find in the Constitution the ringing statements of principle that we find and so often quote from the Declaration of Independence. But the Constitution's most important characteristics are clear and admirable applications of the Natural Law.

Natural Law as understood by the Founding Fathers, and thus the Natural law of the Constitution, was the Natural Law that for two thousand years had been a traditional and essential element of Western Civilization. This would be the Natural law as understood and explained by, for example, Aristotle, Cicero, St. Thomas Aquinas, and John Locke. It was the Founders' traditional understanding of Natural Law.

Cicero said that there is indeed a law, right reason, which is in accordance with nature; existing in all, unchangeable, eternal. It commands us to do what is right, forbidding us to do what is wrong. It has dominion over good men but possesses no influence over bad ones. No other law can be substituted for it, no part of it can be taken away, nor can it be abrogated altogether. Neither the people nor the senate can absolve from it. It is not one thing at Rome, and another thing at Athens: one thing to-day, and another thing tomorrow; but it is eternal and immutable for all nations and for all time.

It is safe to conclude that Cicero did not consider natural law to be akin to a living law that changes as we wish it to change.

The fundamental difference between the classical-traditional understanding of the Natural Law and that of the Enlightenment is that the classical-traditional thinkers knew and declared that God is the author and source of the Natural Law, and that human reason is the faculty by which the Law established by God is made accessible to man. The philosophers of the Enlightenment (who inspired the French Revolution such as Voltaire and Rousseau) rejected God as the author of the Natural Law, or diminished His significance, and elevated human reason, or its variants, such as the general will or a legislative majority, to the position of supremacy or sovereignty.

Limited government thus became the predominant theme of the delegates to the Constitutional Convention. The Natural Law tradition, as stated by its leading exponents and agreed to by Hamilton, Wilson, Madison, and other American founders, holds that the state, and human law, are by nature limited. There are things that government may not do.

The Enlightenment thinkers, either by rejecting God, or by excluding Him from any continuing role in the governance of creation, discarded any principled limitation on the state and government. Human reason ceased to be the faculty by which the law of nature was made known to humans; reason became instead—almost always in some **COLLECTIVIZED** form, such as "the General Will" or "the Nation"—the ultimate source of law itself.

The Constitution reflects the principle of limited government by establishing a national government of enumerated powers. The powers of each branch of the national government are specified, with the necessary implication that all powers not thereby granted, are denied. This critical principle is reaffirmed in the Tenth Amendment. Article I of the Constitution begins by stating:

All legislative powers herein granted shall be vested in a Congress of the United States....

It does not say that "*all* legislative powers shall be vested" in the Congress, but only those legislative powers granted by the Constitution shall be so vested.

Article II begins with the words, "The executive Power shall be vested in a President of the United States of America," but Article II then proceeds to specify the President's powers, thereby limiting executive authority.

Article III, establishing the national judiciary, states that "The Judicial Power of the United States shall extend to" certain specified categories of "cases and controversies," thereby limiting that branch of government as well.

Another indication of the principle of limited government is found in the separation of powers and system of checks and balances outlined in the Constitution.

The second Natural Law principle embedded in the Constitution is the principle of subsidiarity; that is, the principle that government should perform only those tasks not better performed by the family or by private associations; and that, when it *is* appropriate for government to intervene, governmental authority should be exercised by the smallest, most local unit of government capable of effectively performing the task in question. The

Natural Law for this principle is based on the legal theory of St. Thomas Aquinas:

Prior to or independently of any politically organized community, there can exist individuals and families and indeed groups of neighboring families. . .. The family, essentially husband, wife, and children, is antecedent to, and more necessary than, political society.... What is it that solitary individuals, families, and groups of families, inevitably cannot do well? ... Individuals and families cannot well secure and maintain the elements which make up the *public good* of justice and peace ... And so, their instantiation of basic goods is less secure and full than it can be if public justice and peace are maintained by law and other specifically political institutions and activities, in a way that no individual or private group can appropriately undertake or match.

The American understanding of subsidiarity in political affairs is succinctly stated by Lord Bryce:

Where any function can be equally well discharged by a central or by a local body, it ought by preference to be entrusted to the local body, for a central administration is more likely to be tyrannical, inefficient, and impure than one which, being on a small scale, is more fully within the knowledge of the citizens and more sensitive to their opinions.

Subsidiarity has also been defined as a principle of social doctrine that all social bodies exist for the sake of the individual so that what individuals are able to do, society should not take over, and what small societies can do, larger societies should not take over.

While the Constitution did create a national government more powerful than that under the Articles of Confederation, the new government under the United States Constitution continued to be based on the principle of subsidiarity. The debates in Philadelphia demonstrate that the overriding concern of the delegates was the proper allocation of governmental authority between the national government and the States, and the debates that followed in the States over ratification almost always centered on whether the proposed new government would have too much power (leaving the States and the people too little). Almost no one argued that the national government should be given more power than the proposed Constitution allowed.

The Constitution, by enumerating the powers of the various branches of the national government established that all governmental powers not given to the national (or federal) government by the Constitution, belonged to the respective States.

In arguing for the ratification of the Constitution, James Madison emphasized this principle:

The powers delegated by the proposed Constitution to the federal government are few and defined. Those which are to remain in the State governments are numerous and indefinite. The former will be exercised principally on external objects, as war, peace, negotiation, and foreign commerce; with which last the power of taxation will, for the most part, be connected. The powers reserved to the several States will extend to all the objects which, in the ordinary course of affairs; concern the lives, liberties, and properties of the people, and the internal order, improvement, and prosperity of the State.

In addressing a proposal at a later date before Congress to expand the powers of the government beyond the powers specifically delegated within the Constitution, Madison made the following observations: "I, sir, have always conceived—I believe those who proposed the Constitution conceived—it is still more fully known, and more material to observe, that those who ratified the Constitution conceived—that this is not an indefinite government, deriving its powers from the general terms prefixed to the specified powers—but a limited government, tied down to the specified powers, which explain and define the general terms.... "The language held in various discussions of this house is a proof that the doctrine of implied powers in question was never entertained by this body. Arguments, wherever the subject would permit, have constantly been drawn from the peculiar nature of this government, as limited to certain enumerated powers, instead of extending, like other governments, to all cases not particularly excepted.... "In short, sir, without going farther into the subject, which I should not have here touched at all but for the reasons already mentioned, I venture to declare it as my opinion, that, were the power of Congress to be established in the latitude contended for, it would subvert the very foundations, and transmute the very nature of the limited government established by the people of America; and what inferences might be drawn, or what consequences ensue, from such a step, it is incumbent on us all to consider."

To remove any doubt, the principle of subsidiarity, as implied in the original constitutional text, was made explicit in the Tenth Amendment, adopted in 1791:

The powers not delegated to the United States by the Constitution, nor prohibited by it to the States, are reserved to the States respectively or to the people.

The Tenth Amendment thus acknowledges both political subsidiarity—by recognizing that powers are reserved to the States—and subsidiarity in its larger sense—by recognizing that there are powers that do not belong to government at all, but rather are reserved to the people. Thomas Jefferson said the Tenth Amendment was the foundation of the Constitution.

The original text of the Constitution contains few explicit declarations of rights. At the Philadelphia Convention, several delegates had proposed that the document include a charter of rights, but the proposal was unanimously rejected. The principal reason for the rejection was the belief, explained by Hamilton in The Federalist, that the new national government under the Constitution, although it would be more powerful than the government under the Articles, would nevertheless still lack authority to engage in activities that could threaten traditional rights and that, indeed, an enumeration of rights would be counterproductive in that it would support an inference that the national government had more authority than was actually given to it by the Constitution.

During the ratification debates in the States, however, it became evident that much of the opposition to the Constitution was based on fear that the new national government would indeed possess the wherewithal to become oppressive, and that a bill of rights was therefore necessary. As a result, a tacit compromise was reached whereby, if the Constitution were to be ratified, it would be amended to include guarantees of traditional rights.

The Constitution was ratified by the States and entered effect in 1789. The Congress, in its first session, proposed a series of twelve amendments, ten of which were promptly ratified, and have long been known collectively as the Bill of Rights.

The First Amendment reads as follows:

Congress shall make **NO LAW** respecting an establishment of religion or prohibiting the free exercise thereof; or **ABRIDGING** the freedom of speech, or of the press; or the right of the people peaceably to assemble, and to petition the Government for a redress of grievances.

It is significant that the First Amendment does not pretend to create the freedoms and rights referred to; quite the contrary. The language of the Amendment clearly implies that these freedoms and rights have existed prior to and independent of their mention in the Constitution, and that the only reason for including them in the Constitution is to make certain that the new national government will not violate them.

Like the Tenth Amendment that clarifies the role of national government as subservient to the people, the Ninth Amendment clarifies that there are other rights that may exist aside from the ones explicitly mentioned, and even though they are not listed, it does not mean they can be violated.

The Ninth Amendment: The enumeration in the Constitution, of certain rights, shall not be construed to deny or disparage others retained by the people.

The founders clearly intended that the United States would be an individualist nation as opposed to a collectivist nation. Individualism is the idea that the individual's life belongs to themselves and that each has an unalienable right to live it as each sees fit, to act on their own judgment, to keep and use the product of their effort, and to pursue the values of their choosing. It's the idea that the individual is sovereign, an end unto them self, and the fundamental unit of moral concern.

Collectivism is the idea that the individual's life belongs not to each person but to the group or society of which each is merely a part, that each has no rights, and that each must sacrifice their values and goals for the group's "greater good." According to collectivism, the group or society is the basic unit of moral concern, and the individual is of value only insofar as each serves the group. As collectivist Maurice Low stated, "Man has no rights except those which society permits him to enjoy. From the day of his birth until the day of his death society allows him to enjoy certain so-called rights and deprives him of others; not . . . because society desires to favor or oppress the individual, but because its own preservation, welfare, and happiness are the prime considerations."

The founders also understood that to remain free the United States must remain a nation that continues to adhere to "rule of law," remains a nation with a "limited government," insures that the government is always a "divided government," and that the government continue to be the servant to a "sovereign people."

WE CHOSE LOCKE

THE DECLARATION OF INDEPENDENCE STATES, "WE HOLD THESE TRUTHS TO BE SELF EVIDENT, THAT ALL MEN ARE CREATED EQUAL AND THEY ARE ENDOWED BY THEIR CRATOR WITH CERTAIN UNALIENALBE RIGHTS, AMONGST THESE THE RIGHT TO LIFE, LIBERTY, AND THE PURSUIT OF HAPPINESS."

Sam Adams stated in November of 1772, "Among the natural rights of the Colonists are these: First, a right to life; Secondly, to liberty; Thirdly, to property; together with the right to support and defend them in the best manner they can. These are evident branches of, rather than deductions from, the duty of self-preservation, commonly called the first law of nature."

In both statements we are told that man has natural rights of life and liberty. Sam Adams also states that property is a natural right of man, quoting this directly from John Locke. Thomas Jefferson, in the Declaration of Independence, does not use the term property, but instead extends the definition of property per Adams and Locke, to conform to the capitalist economy of the colonists. Jefferson says a natural right of man is the right of an individual to pursue their own happiness and not be constrained in their pursuits by the dictates of others including the dictates of government. Most importantly perhaps is that Locke, Adams, and Jefferson all understood that these natural rights are given to everyone, by the Creator, as an individual and not as a part of a collective. Since these natural rights are given to the individual by the Creator, who is sovereign overall, neither man nor government have the right to limit these natural rights of life, liberty, and property, which includes the pursuit of happiness.

Since the time of the ancient Greeks, people have argued in support of the existence of natural rights, meaning those rights that men possessed as a gift from the Creator prior to the formation of governments. It was widely held that those rights belonged equally to all men at conception and could not be taken away by man nor government.

John Locke argued that man was originally born into a state of nature where he was rational, tolerant, and happy. In this original existence man was entitled to enjoy the rights of life, liberty and property. However, Locke continued, not all men chose to live within the confines of the natural laws and presented threats to the liberties of others. Because of this, man entered into a social contract (compact) in which a state (government) was formed to protect these natural rights of the members of society. Locke believed that the only reason for the existence of government was to preserve natural rights and, by extension, man's happiness and security. Locke did not advocate that the government was to assume the role of granting natural rights and by extension guaranteeing man's happiness and security.

Jefferson asserted in the Declaration of Independence that the pursuit of happiness was strictly a function of the individual and not a function of nor a responsibility of the state or government. Jefferson extended this idea when he stated that government is an entity created by the people for the benefit of the people. Since government received its right to function from the people, the people would thus be the sovereign and the government would be the servant.

"GOVERNMENTS ARE INSTITUTED AMONGST MEN AND RECEIVE THEIR JUST POWER FROM THE CONSENT OF THE GOVERNED."

Natural right is the belief that certain rights exist independently of any government's granting of those rights. The general phrase has been life, liberty, and property or the pursuit of happiness. These phrases are used so often that we forget to stop to think what they mean. An individual's right to life is beyond the will of the government except in the instance of an individual violating the natural right to life of another. As Locke stated, government was formed to not give rights but to protect rights. A part of the protection of the right to life is the surrendering of a person's own life when they violate the natural right to life of another. If the government did not protect this right, society would be at the risk of rampant and condoned murder for personal gain.

In a totalitarian state, the government has determined that it is the sovereign. Being sovereign, the government than assumes the role that all life is not a natural right, but a right granted by the government. The twentieth century was a horrific example of government assuming the role of sovereign and determining who and for what reason classes of people had the right to life. Millions upon millions of individuals had their natural right to life taken from them by collectivist governments in Russia later the Soviet Union, members of the Soviet Bloc, China, Nazi Germany, Cuba, and many others.

The English Oxford Dictionary defines liberty as the state of being free within society from oppressive restrictions imposed by authority on one's way of life, behavior, or political views. Serfs in different societies had no liberty. Their life was determined even prior to their conception. There life would be at the mercy of another, their work was pre-destined, who they could marry must be approved by another. Their education level, if any, was determined by others. They were not allowed to have political views. Even their speech and their thoughts were controlled by others. They had no liberty.

The right to property extends beyond the common view of property as being only real estate or some other tangible. Under natural rights, the right to property was extended by Thomas Jefferson to include the right to pursue happiness. Jefferson extended property rights to an individual's desired educational level, artistic capabilities, and even economic desires and ambitions which would extend property under natural law to income, both present and future.

Life, liberty, and property or pursuit of happiness are very broad. The founders were concerned that a broad rather than a narrow interpretation be applied. To assure this, they added the Ninth amendment to the Bill of Rights.

Ninth Amendment: **"THE ENUMERATION IN THE CONSTITUTION OF CERTAIN RIGHTS, SHALL NOT BE CONSTRUED TO DENY OR DISPARAGE OTHERS RETAINED BY THE PEOPLE."** What this means is that there are other rights that may exist aside from the ones explicitly mentioned, and even though they are not listed, it does not mean they can be violated by man or government.

The First Amendment is very specific about additional natural rights of people. These rights as outlined in the First Amendment are at the very heart of maintaining the free, open, and individualist nation designed by our founders; a nation with a limited government that adheres to the concept that natural rights must always be secure. The First Amendment states: **"CONGRESS SHALL MAKE NO LAW RESPECTING AN ESTABLISHMENT OF RELIGION OR PROHIBITING THE FREE EXERCISE THEREOF; OR ABRIDGING THE FREEDOM OF SPEECH, OR OF THE PRESS; OR THE RIGHT OF THE PEOPLE PEACEBLY TO ASSEMBLE, AND TO PETITION THE GOVERNMENT FOR A REDRESS OF GRIEVANCES."**

The founders understood that these rights are natural rights granted by the ultimate sovereign, the Creator, and therefore neither man nor government had any roll in granting them and could not limit them in any form. The amendment says that Congress shall make **NO** law abridging; which means Congress does not have the right to restrict any element of these freedoms which would include limiting the right of speech by defining hate speech and then limit accordingly.

John Locke is one of the founders of "liberal" political philosophy, the philosophy of individual rights and limited government. This is the philosophy on which the American Constitution and some other Western political systems today are based. In the "Second Treatise of Government," commonly thought to be Locke's most important political work, he uses natural law to ground his philosophy. But there are many different interpretations of the natural law, from the Ciceronian to the Thomistic. What is Locke's interpretation? What version of natural law supports "liberal" politics?

Some argue that this is a misguided question. They say that Locke's political philosophy is not based on natural law at all, but instead on natural rights, like the philosophy of Thomas Hobbes. Natural law theories hold that human beings are subject to a moral law. Morality is fundamentally about duty, the duty the individual must abide by the natural law. Thomas Hobbes created a new approach when he based morality not on duty but on right, the individual's right to preserve himself, to pursue his own good—essentially, to do as he wishes.

Is Locke a follower of Hobbes, basing his theory on right rather than natural law? What difference does it make? One characteristic of a rights theory is that it takes man to be by nature a solitary and independent creature, as in Hobbes's "state of nature." In Hobbes's "state of nature," men are free and independent, having a right to pursue their own self-interest, and no duties to one another. The moral logic is something like this: nature has made individuals independent; nature has left the individual to fend for himself; nature must therefore have granted each person a right to fend for himself. This right is the fundamental moral fact, rather than any duty individuals have to a law or to each other. The priority of individual right reflects our separateness, our lack of moral ties to one another. According to Hobbes, one consequence of this is that the state of nature is a "war of all against all": human beings are naturally at war with one another. Individuals create societies and governments to escape this condition. Society is not natural to man, but is the product of a "social contract," a contract to which each separate individual must consent. The sole purpose of the contract is to safeguard the rights of each citizen.

This is the basic recipe for the political philosophy of liberalism—Locke's philosophy, the primary philosophy upon which the United States was founded. Locke speaks of a state of nature where men are free, equal, and independent. He champions the social contract and government by consent. He goes even farther than Hobbes in arguing that government must respect the rights of individuals. It was Locke's formula for limited government, more than Hobbes's, that inspired the American Founding Fathers. But what is the basis of Locke's theory, natural law or Hobbesian natural right? The Founding Fathers, in the Declaration of Independence, speak of both natural rights and natural laws. Locke does likewise. Natural law and natural right may be combined, but if they are, one must take precedence over the other. Either the individual's right, or his duty to moral law, must come first.

Locke's position is clarified in Chapter Two of the "Second Treatise of Government," where Locke asserts that men in the state of nature are free and equal, and at liberty to do as they wish—but only "within the bounds of the law of nature." This limitation separates Locke from Hobbes. Hobbes had argued that freedom and equality, and the priority of individual right, meant that individuals in the state of nature could pursue their survival and interest without limitation. They had no duty to respect the rights of others. Therefore, the state of nature was a state of war. Locke's claim is that individuals have a duty to respect the rights of others, even in the state of nature. The source of this duty, he says, is natural law.

The difference with Hobbes is clearest in Locke's argument about property. Hobbes and Locke agree that individuals have a right to property in the state of nature, but Hobbes denies that individuals have any duty to respect the property of others. This makes property useless in Hobbes's state of nature. Locke says individuals have a duty to respect the property (and lives and liberties) of others even in the state of nature, a duty he traces to natural law. Natural law and natural rights coexist, but natural law is primary, commanding respect for the rights of others.

Here, then, is the issue in the natural law–natural right dichotomy: if individual right is primary, can individuals have any duty to respect the rights of others? If the fundamental moral fact is the individual's right to "look out for number one," where would a duty to respect others come from? Hobbes finds no such duty, for it would restrict the individual's liberty and his right. Locke argues for a duty to respect others' rights, but traces it to natural law, not right. Locke's view is the view most of us share—I have rights, but "my right to swing my fist ends where your nose begins." We typically think of individual rights as being coupled with a responsibility to respect the rights of others. Locke's argument suggests that this responsibility depends upon duty and natural law, not individual right, as the basis of morality.

Or does it? There is a potentially serious loophole in Locke's argument. In Chapter Two of the Second Treatise, he says that the individual only has a duty to respect others' rights when "his own preservation comes not in competition." If my life is threatened, I need not respect anyone else's rights, I may do whatever is necessary to preserve myself. How extensive is this loophole? If the state of nature is as violent and desperate as Hobbes said it was, with everyone under continual threat of death, Locke's duty to respect the rights of others would essentially vanish.

Some have argued that this is Locke's true meaning. In the beginning of the Second Treatise, Locke seems to claim that the state of nature is a place of peace and harmony. Later, however, he makes it clear that the state of nature was actually very insecure, with people's rights under continual threat. Conditions "drive" men to form a social contract for their protection. If Locke's state of nature is as violent as Hobbes's, it could mean that Locke's natural duty to respect others amounts to little or nothing, that the individual's right to fend for himself is primary after all, and that Locke is much closer to Hobbes than he seems. He might want us to think, as some Locke scholars have argued, that he is a traditional natural law thinker, while conveying a secret, "esoteric" teaching based squarely on Hobbes's individual right instead.

This is the deepest controversy in Locke interpretation today, a controversy that is sometimes acrimonious. Even for those who see Locke as a kind of Hobbesian, though, it is generally agreed that Locke believes in some degree of natural duty to respect the rights of others. In this view, Locke's argument is based on rights rather than law, but he understands the rights differently:

perhaps rights imply reciprocity, or mutual respect among individuals, in a way that Hobbes failed to see. Similarly, for those who see Locke as a natural law thinker, there is controversy over the source of that law. Locke says, in the First Treatise of Government and elsewhere, that God is the source of the natural law. But God is much less in evidence in the Second Treatise. What is Locke's view? Further, if Locke is serious about natural law, it is clear that his version of natural law is quite different from that of other natural law thinkers, such as Thomas Aquinas. Locke's natural law sanctions the basic right of individuals to pursue their own self-interest—to accumulate wealth, for example. If Locke is a natural law thinker, his version of natural law is much more individualistic, much closer to Hobbes, than were previous versions.

For present-day Americans, one reason for studying Locke (together with Hobbes) is to understand the character of liberalism. A liberal system such as ours, based on individual rights, but its health depends upon people exercising those rights responsibly. It depends on people taking seriously their duty to respect the rights of others.

Many observers believe that, while Americans today are eager to claim their rights, too few are willing to shoulder the attendant responsibilities. Is a rights-based society doomed to degenerate into simple selfishness? Or is it possible to construct a rights philosophy with a robust element of responsibility built into it? Must such a philosophy place natural law above individual right? Must this law have a religious dimension? These are questions that should send us back to Hobbes, Locke, and the architects of the American Constitution.

If causing trouble was the goal of the Founding Fathers in 1776, attacking the notion that rulers derived their authority to govern from the Divine Right of Kings was certainly the way to go.

The governments of the most powerful nations on Earth pushed the idea that their kings were chosen directly by God and that their authority, therefore, could not be questioned, nor could the people hold their kings accountable for their actions. Kings, as alleged representatives of God, therefore, were not subject to any earthly authority, certainly not to the people or even the aristocracy of their kingdoms. They were, in a very real sense, above the laws of man and answerable only to God, Himself.

Washington, Jefferson, Adams and the other troublemakers in America had a different view, however. They believed that rulers gained their legitimacy from the consent of the governed and from Natural Law, a system of laws of morality, derived from the natural order of things to which all humans are ethically bound.

No public document gives more prominence to the idea of natural law, nor relies more crucially upon natural law as a premise, than the Declaration of Independence," wrote Dr. James R. Stoner, Jr., professor and head of the political science department at Louisiana State University. He cites, as an example, the most famous passage from the Declaration:

"We hold these truths to be self-evident: That all men are created equal; that they are endowed by their Creator with certain unalienable rights; that among these are life, liberty and the pursuit of happiness; that, to secure these rights, governments are instituted among men, deriving their just powers from the consent of the governed; that whenever any form of government becomes destructive of these ends, it is the right of the people to abolish it, and to institute new government, laying its foundation on such principles, and organizing its powers in such form, as to them shall seem more likely to affect their safety and happiness."

Our nation was founded on the premise that we the people have natural rights that were given to us by the Creator. The only role government has regarding these rights is to protect these rights. Government did not grant these rights and therefore has no right in controlling or abridging in any form. However, we, the people, have a duty and responsibility to adhere to this system of natural laws of morality and ethics.

BILL OF RIGHTS DEMANDED

The Constitutional Convention in Philadelphia met between May and September of 1787 to address the problems of the weak central government that existed under the Articles of Confederation. Under the Articles of Confederation, the federal government faced many challenges in conducting foreign policy, largely due to its inability to pass or enforce laws that individual states found counter to their interests. The Constitutional Convention was called together under the pretense that changes should be made to the Articles of Confederation. Changes were made you might say. A completely new document was drafted called the Constitution of the United States.

The original Constitution, as proposed and as ratified by the states, contained very few individual rights guarantees, as the framers were primarily focused on establishing the machinery for an effective federal government. A proposal by delegate Charles Pinckney to include several rights guarantees was submitted to the Committee on Detail on August 20, 1787, but the Committee did not adopt any of Pinckney's recommendations. The matter came before the Convention on September 12, 1787, and, following a brief debate, proposals to include a Bill or Rights in the Constitution were rejected. As adopted, the Constitution included only a few specific rights guarantees: protection against states impairing the obligation of contracts, provisions that prohibit both the federal and state governments from enforcing ex post facto laws (laws that allow punishment for an action that was not criminal at the time it was undertaken) and provisions barring bills of attainder (legislative determinations of guilt and punishment). The framers, and notably James Madison, its principal architect, believed that the Constitution protected liberty primarily through its division of powers that made it difficult for an oppressive majority to form and capture power to be used against minorities. Delegates also probably feared that a debate over liberty guarantees might prolong or even threaten the fiercely debated compromises that had been made over the long hot summer of 1787.

In the ratification debate, Anti-Federalists opposed to the Constitution, complained that the new system threatened liberties, and suggested that if the delegates had truly cared about protecting individual rights, they would have included provisions in the Constitution that accomplished that. With ratification in serious doubt, Federalists, Hamilton's party, announced a willingness to entertain the matter of a series of amendments, to be called the Bill of Rights, soon after ratification and the First Congress came into session. The concession was necessary to insure the Constitution's hard-fought ratification. Thomas Jefferson, who did not attend the Constitutional Convention, in a December 1787 letter to Madison called the omission of a Bill of Rights a major mistake: "A bill of rights is what the people are entitled to against every government on earth."

James Madison was skeptical of the value of a listing of rights, calling it a "parchment barrier." Despite his skepticism, by the fall of 1788, Madison believed that a declaration of rights should be added to the Constitution. Its value, in Madison's view, was in part educational, in part as a vehicle that might be used to rally people against a future oppressive government, and finally--in an argument borrowed from Thomas Jefferson--

Madison argued that a declaration of rights would help install the judiciary as "guardians" of individual rights against the other branches. When the First Congress met in 1789, James Madison, a congressman from Virginia, took upon himself the task of drafting a proposed Bill of Rights. His original set of proposed amendments included some that were either rejected or substantially modified by Congress, and one (dealing with apportionment of the House) that was not ratified by the required three-fourths of the state legislatures. Some of the rejections were very significant, such as the decision not to adopt Madison's proposal to extend free speech protections to the states, and others somewhat less important, perhaps.

Some members of Congress argued that a listing of rights of the people was a silly exercise, in that all the listed rights inherently belonged to citizens, and nothing in the Constitution gave the Congress the power to take them away. It was even suggested that the Bill of Rights might reduce liberty by giving force to the argument that all rights not specifically listed could be infringed upon. In part to counter this concern, the Ninth

Amendment was included providing that "The enumeration in the Constitution of certain rights, shall not be construed to deny or disparage other rights retained by the people." Decades later, the Ninth Amendment would be pointed to by some judges, as a justification for giving a broad and liberty-protective reading to the specifically enumerated rights.

In the end, we owe opponents of the Constitution a debt of gratitude, for without their complaints, there would be no Bill of Rights. Thomas Jefferson wrote, "There has just been opposition enough" to force adoption of a Bill of Rights, but not to drain the federal government of its essential "energy." George Washington agreed: "They have given the rights of man a full and fair discussion and explained them in so clear and forcible manner as cannot fail to make a lasting impression."

A strong consensus amongst our founders was that freedom of speech, in the first amendment, is absolutely critical if the society and government for which they fought the Revolutionary War and the society they envisioned under the Constitution recently drafted and ratified was to exist; that society was a society with a limited government that did not intrude into nor dictate the lives and thoughts of its citizens. This dedication to freedom of speech was expressed in later times as well.

Following are direct quotes reinforcing how critical freedom of speech is to freedom and reasons why.

"But freedom of speech and of the press – no matter how much we may disagree with and even hate what someone else says – is the bedrock of America." George Washington

"If freedom of speech is taken away, then dumb and silent we may be led, like sheep to the slaughter." George Washington

"Freedom of speech is a principal pillar of a free government: When this support is taken away, the constitution of a free society is dissolved, and tyranny is erected on its ruins." Ben Franklin

"Without freedom of thought, there can be no such thing as wisdom; and no such thing as public liberty, without freedom of speech." Ben Franklin

"Whoever would overthrow the liberty of a nation must begin by subduing the freeness of speech." Ben Franklin

"The power to censor, more than any other, ought to produce universal alarm, because it is levelled against that right of freely examining public characters and measures, and of free communication among the people thereon, which has ever been justly deemed, the only effectual guardian of every other right." James Madison

"If there is any principle of the Constitution that more imperatively calls for attachment than any other it is the principle of free thought — not free thought for those who agree with us but freedom for the thought that we hate." U.S. Supreme Court Justice Oliver Wendell Holmes Jr.

"Freedom of expression is the matrix, the indispensable condition, of nearly every other form of freedom." U.S. Supreme Court Justice Benjamin Cardozo

"The framers of the constitution knew human nature as well as we do. They too had lived in dangerous days; they too knew the suffocating influence of orthodoxy and standardized thought. They weighed the compulsions for restrained speech and thought against the abuses of liberty. They chose liberty." U.S. Supreme Court Justice William Douglass

"If there be time to expose through discussion the falsehood and fallacies, to avert the evil by the processes of education, the remedy to be applied is more speech, not enforced silence." U.S. Supreme Court Justice Louis D. Brandeis

That is why the priority for all totalitarian regimes was and is to impose restrictions on freedom of speech. In 1917, the Russian Bolsheviks moved to limit freedom of speech the very day after the October coup-d'état. They adopted the "Decree on the Press," which shut down any newspapers "sowing discord by libelous distortion of facts." Lenin wrote that, "to tolerate the existence of these newspapers means to cease to be a socialist." Similarly, only a few months after coming to power in 1933, German National Socialists started to burn books, and the Ministry of Propaganda introduced strict censorship.

Modern dictators and leaders of totalitarian states have also learned all too well that freedom of speech is their worst enemy that eventually precipitates collapse of despotic regimes. Today the bottom rankings in press freedom ratings are occupied by such communist countries as China, Cuba, North Korea, Vietnam, as well as ideologically divergent, but equally harsh despotic regimes, such as Turkmenistan, Belarus, Iran, Syria, Sudan, and others.

States that lean towards totalitarian methods of governance need to create a strong propaganda machine designed to replace reliable information, policy analysis, and a free exchange of views. Intrusive government propaganda can create an image of an external or internal enemy, drastically distort the real picture of the world and the course of current events, awaken feelings of xenophobia and racial or national exclusiveness, and manipulate people's minds.

Article 5 of the Articles of Confederation stated:

Delegates' freedom of speech is protected while they are serving in Congress. Delegates may not be arrested or put in prison while they are in Congress, or traveling to and from, unless they have committed treason, a felony, or have been guilty of breach of the peace.

The Ninth and Tenth amendments are critical to liberty for American citizens. The Ninth Amendment offers a constitutional safety net, intended to make it clear that Americans have other fundamental rights beyond those listed in the Bill of Rights. The amendment was added out of concern that it would be impossible to mention every fundamental right, and dangerous to list just some of them for fear of suggesting that the list was complete. Because the rights protected by the amendment are not specified, they are referred to as "unenumerated" rights, as opposed to those enumerated.

The Tenth Amendment was included in the Bill of Rights to preserve the balance of power between the federal government and the states. The amendment limits the federal government's power to just what is written in the Constitution. Those powers not listed are left to each of the states. The Tenth Amendment does not specify what those "powers" are. The powers of the federal government would be referred to as "enumerated" rights.

It is critical to understand that all rights protected are rights and not entitlements. The exercise of any of these rights by an individual is not contingent on another individual having his rights reduced or eliminated. All these rights are natural rights and it is the sole role of government to protect these rights and not restrict or eliminate them in any manner.

RIGHTS IN THE DECLARATION OF INDEPENDENCE

In 1776 a people known as American Colonists revolted against the British King, King George III, insisting he had violated their natural rights. The document describing these rights and the King's violations was titled the "Declaration of Independence." Not only was this a declaration of independence, but it should also be construed to be a declaration of war, a declaration of war against an entity with a vastly superior military.

This Declaration has inspired many through the subsequent years, decades, and centuries. It is truly astonishing that a document written over 240 years ago can still hold relevance, yet the words of the Declaration of Independence are as relevant today as they were in 1776. The Thirteen United States of America, as they named themselves in the official document issued to the King, sought to define liberty, freedom, and equality as they saw them. They demanded economic and political independence from King George and the British Empire.

Historically, a "declaration" has been a "public document issued by a representative body." Legally, in a civil trial, it is a "form in which the plaintiff sets forth his cause of complaint at length." In diplomacy, a declaration is a "formal international announcement by an official body, either by a general manifesto published to all the world; or by a note to each particular court, delivered by an ambassador."

These definitions give us a better understanding of the intent behind the document. The Declaration as an international manifesto was not a novel concept, but the assertions and accusations it presented were extraordinary. The phrase "let facts be submitted to a candid world" reveal the awareness the Continental Congress had of the international attention declaring independence would bring to the United States. Therefore, it can be assumed that the Declaration of Independence was a document publicly and internationally issued to announce the crimes of King George III and to assert the sovereignty of the Thirteen United States.

The phrase "we hold these truths to be self-evident that all men are created equal," has been debated and is perhaps the most misunderstood of all the phrases in the Declaration of Independence; perhaps in all our founding documents. Jefferson stated this is a truth and should be self-evident to all. Yet, many have said this means Americans should be financially equal, even though that is an ending and not a beginning as created would indicate. We also know equality does not refer to abilities or capabilities either physically or mentally. The truth that people are physically and mentally different, even at birth, is self-evident.

What was self-evident is that people are created with equal opportunity regardless of their designated position at birth. In England and Europe in the 18th Century, there was a distinct difference between the classes, nobility and commoner. Opportunities open to the nobility were not available to the commoner. For instance, officers in the military were members of the nobility, and a commoner, despite ability, would be passed over for the member of the nobility. There were definite classes of nobility and commoners, and they were not considered to be equal or to have equal opportunity. This would be different in America, according to the Declaration of Independence, because in America it was a truth and self-evident that all were created equal.

Natural rights are then mentioned but they are not explained because as Jefferson wrote, they were self-evident and an explanation of them was unnecessary. History shows that the natural rights and natural law explained by John Locke, had been a topic of conversation for many years. Sam Adams referred to the natural rights of live, liberty, and property in November of 1772. The Declaration says that men are "endowed by their Creator with certain unalienable rights that among these are life, liberty, and the pursuit of happiness." Jefferson substituted "pursuit of happiness" for property. This in no way eliminates property as a natural right but instead expands property to the abilities and capabilities leading to the desires or pursuits of the individual as a part of their natural rights.

These natural rights are given by the Creator. Rights cannot be given by two different entities. Our founding document that declared we would be independent from the tyrannical government of the King, also declares that our natural rights are not granted by man nor government. Government was thus placed in a subservient position. Because our natural rights are given by the Creator, the only role government would have regarding rights, would be as the protector of those rights. Government would not have the authority to restrict or control those rights.

The rights of man are natural rights. The three rights commonly mentioned and included in the Declaration of Independence are only "among" the natural rights of man. This clearly insinuates the list extends beyond what is stated. This ambiguity allows for the list of natural rights to be augmented in future discussions and for the rights that are listed to be defined as necessary in future interpretations. This same argument is accentuated by the addition of the Ninth Amendment to the Bill of Rights that is also discussed in this book. This same reasoning would also insinuate that the rights mentioned were natural and the acts of the King or government were unnatural, invoking the sense of right and wrong.

Arthur Young, * only four years prior to July 1776 wrote that "liberty is the natural birthright of mankind and yet to take a comprehensive view of the world, how few enjoy it." His statement illustrates how liberty and equality, as many define equality today, are at odds with one another. Liberty creates opportunity but equality hinders it. Liberty allows for people to obtain an education, to be trained in a profession of their choice, to live where they choose, to spend their earnings how they deem fit. Liberty creates different levels in society based on success of people in exercising the opportunity liberty created. Equality, again based on how it is used by many today, prevents total liberty. Equality does not allow for any one person to be in a better or worse position than another even though one person may excel at one task while a second person does not. True equality denies the excellent person from claiming their superiority at a task. Jefferson listed liberty as a natural right, but equality was not. Instead, equality was a self-evident truth. Truths can be disputed and denied because they are of man. Natural rights are given by the Creator and to deny them would be to deny the natural order as God intended it to be.

In his second treatise on government, John Locke rhetorically questions "how much better a monarchy is than the state of nature where one man commanding a multitude has the liberty to be judge in his own case and may do to all his subjects whatever he pleases without the least liberty to anyone to question or control those who execute his pleasure."

Locke views monarchies the same as did Jefferson in his treatment of George III in the Declaration. The list of "injuries and usurpations" Jefferson makes addresses the ways in which the King attempted to establish his tyranny over the colonists. Jefferson's list seems to be Locke's fears come to fruition. According to Jefferson in the Declaration, the King paid no mind to the rights and wishes of his subjects but rather made decisions in order to further his desires and interests thus committing the crime Locke cited as the reason people form governments; to protect themselves from "confusion and disorder" that follows men being the judge in their own case or punishing others too ruthlessly.

The list of the King's transgressions begins with specific acts of King George, but it morphs into a purposefully unspecific list of allegations to allow it to apply to other situations and hopefully inspire others to rise against any tyrannical state. The crimes of any tyrannical state would read the same.

The Americans in the Declaration charged George with several crimes. Among these crimes were George's refusal to "assent to laws, the most wholesome and necessary for the public good...for taking away our charters, abolishing our most valuable laws, and altering fundamentally the forms of our governments... abdicating government here, by declaring us out of his protection and waging war against us...for plundering our seas, ravaging our Coasts, burning our towns, and destroying the lives of our people."

The accusations did not stop with the King. The Declaration also sites those they considered their "British brethren" and found them guilty of being "deaf to the voice of justice and of consanguinity," (the fact of being descended from the same ancestor). We can surmise this phrase was the result of carefully selecting words. The Continental Congress replaced a version of Jefferson's original accusations in order to not offend those British citizens who were sympathetic to the American struggle for independence.

This type of deliberate vagueness of the language can also be found when it is stated that "whenever any form of government becomes destructive...it is the right of the people to alter or abolish it and to institute new government laying its foundation on such principles." The elusiveness of this statement is great but at the same time, the statement can be seen as specific. It is specific in terms of the situation it describes. That is, it references the situation as being that of a political struggle rather than an ethical or cultural one. It can also apply to a variety of states at a variety of times because of the use of "any form of government" and "the right of the people."

These phrases suggest that any state, be it tyrannical or democratic, is temporary and conditional based on its citizens opinions. Governments are made by people in order to, at the most fundamental level, provide them with security. It is when the government becomes a greater threat to the people's security than it is a provider of security that it becomes necessary for the people to abolish such a government.

The divineness of leadership then becomes obsolete, dissolving the centuries old claim to power and establishing another natural right of man, the right to participation in and a voice in one's government in the interest of security. The Declaration put forth this power to alter or abolish a destructive government to appeal to people, to the colonists at that time, and to all people in future times.

The war that followed the adopting of the Declaration was a battle for freedom and independence, a battle for self-government, and an economic battle which the American states had every intention of winning, despite the heavy odds against that happening.

Without political freedom, the colonists would not have been able to demand economic independence. The economic struggle as the colonists saw it, is made clear in the list of the

King's transgressions when it is stated that the King was guilty of "cutting off our trade with all parts of the world, for imposing taxes on us without our consent" as well as in the conclusion of the document when it is said that "as free and independent states they have full power to levy war, conclude peace, contract alliances, establish commerce, and to do all other acts and things which independent states may of right do."

As an independent nation, the United States would have freedom to exercise their right as a nation to, among other things, practice commerce as they wish. The infringement of a nation's economic freedom could be viewed as grounds for warfare, so in declaring their autonomy as an independent nation, the United States hoped that their economic interests would be protected and in their own control.

The Declaration was in many ways a manifesto on the natural rights of the individual and the role of government in its citizen's lives. The Declaration's call for the natural rights of the individual was perhaps overwhelmed by the call for states' rights and autonomy. This cannot, however, diminish the importance of the natural rights of the individual the Declaration advocates.

The motives of the colonists may have been mixed, as motives in many situations tend to be and the fact that money was a factor does not discredit the character of those men in the Continental Congress. Those men that signed the Declaration were risking everything they owned and their lives. Their act of valor was a demonstration of their confidence in the principles set forth in the document. To prove they knew the risks they were taking, they mutually pledged their "lives, fortunes, and sacred honor" and signed their names beneath that pledge demonstrating their understanding of their actions. The odds of them prevailing were very limited given the fact that Great Britain had a powerful Army and Navy and the financial resources to support them. The colonists did not have a Navy, they had what has been described as a "rag tag" army, and they had very limited financial resources.

According to 19th century American politician, Peleg Sprague, the individual rights mentioned in the Declaration were to inform a "whole people, of what before existed, and will always exist, the native equality of the human race, as the true foundation of all political, of all human institutions." The invocation of equality was necessary and influenced the thirteen new states in the drafting of their new state Constitutions and Bill of Rights. This can be attributed to two reasons. First, the men writing the state Constitutions were the same men who had either written the Declaration or revised and edited it so naturally similarities would exist. The second reason being that many of the states believed in equality, an ideal that could be traced back to religious values and Enlightenment influences, especially in the New England states. The Virginia State Declaration of 1776 stated that "all men are by nature equally free and independent and have certain inherent rights," the Pennsylvania State Declaration of 1776 stated that "all men are born equally free and independent and have certain natural, inherent and inalienable rights" and the Massachusetts State Constitution of 1780 in its first sentence said that "all men are born free and equal, and have certain natural, essential, and unalienable rights; among which may be reckoned the right of enjoying and defending their lives and liberties." Individual rights were immediately accepted by the states as a central part of the new government they were consenting to become a part of by signing the Declaration of Independence. Wealth alone was not enough to risk dying for, but equality and individual rights that were natural and therefore irrevocable were principles worth the risk of death.

The version of the Declaration that is preserved today is the final version that was ratified and passed by the Continental Congress in 1776. The process used by the members of the Continental Congress serves as the first example of the British colonies cooperating as the United States in an internationally official political capacity. Thomas Jefferson's original draft of the Declaration was revised and edited by the other members of the Continental Congress in order to create a document on which all parties agreed. This goal required compromise and can also account for the vague language of the document, but it also accounts for the elasticity of the language as well. In large groups it is difficult, if not impossible, to grant the exact wishes of each member, compromise allows for all members to be satisfied.

In the Declaration compromise emerges as elastic language. In the opening paragraph the phrase "dissolve the political bands" is used, the choice to use this phrase demonstrates the elastic nature of the document.

The suggestion of colonialism as a political band not only reduces the power of the King of England in theory but also suggests that all governments are merely bonds between the ruler and those being ruled. The term band indicates peoples or groups working together for a common outcome that separate once the outcome has been achieved. It does not include dominance of one group or persons over the other nor does it allude to non-mutual cooperation. The phrase, as its written in the Declaration, could apply to any variety of political affiliations in which the governed feel oppressed because it is not a specific identification of the colonial relationship between America and Great Britain.

Later in the document, before the list of the King's injuries and usurpations, it is stated that it is the right of the people to "provide new guards for their future security." This statement is not expanded upon, the type of guard to be provided is not explicitly mentioned, nor is what exactly constitutes security defined. Perhaps this is because the writers were unsure of the definitions or it is because not defining the terms would allow for the document to be ratified and signed by more representatives. Not defining the terms suggested that states would be able to define these terms on their own as was fit for their population. After all, the colonies did not necessarily view themselves as a country, but rather as a union of individual states fighting for a common purpose. Thus, each state would provide for its future security in its own way so to define it in the Declaration would be unnecessary. Unclear selection of language provides a timeless nature to the Declaration and allows for more people and groups to relate to the document concludes Peleg Sprague.

* Arthur Young, (born Sept. 11, 1741, London, Eng.—died April 20, 1820, London), prolific English writer on agriculture, politics, and economics.

RIGHTS IN THE CONSTITUTION

We commonly hear the comment, "that is my constitutional right." This is a not a comment based on literal rights granted by the Constitution but holds merit only because of the spirit of the Constitution and has even more meaning when the Declaration of Independence and Bill of Rights are considered. The fundamental meaning of the U. S. Constitution depends on the proper understanding of Natural Rights belonging to every citizen. The U.S. government is the first and only government in history to be founded on Natural Law. Even though nothing is mentioned in the Constitution about Natural Law, the document sometimes referred to as the "spirit" of the Constitution does; that spirit is the Declaration of Independence.

The Constitution as it came from the Philadelphia convention contained no bill of rights. Indeed, the word right (or rights) appears only once in it, and there only in the context of Congress's power to promote the progress of science and useful arts "by securing for limited Times to Authors and Inventors the exclusive Right to their respective Writings and

Discoveries" (Article 1, section 8). In the view of the Anti-Federalists, the Constitution should have begun with a statement of general principles, or of "admirable maxims," as Patrick Henry said in the Virginia ratifying debates, such as the statement in the Virginia declaration of rights of 1776 declares: "That all men are by nature equally free and independent, and have certain inherent rights, of which, when they enter a state of society, they cannot by any compact deprive or divest their posterity; namely, the enjoyment of life and liberty, with the means of acquiring and possessing property, and pursuing and obtaining happiness and safety." In short, a bill of rights ought to be affixed to the Constitution containing a statement of natural rights, so said the Anti-Federalists.

The Federalists disagreed. They conceded that the Constitution might properly contain a statement of civil rights, and they were instrumental in the adoption of the first ten amendments which we know as the Bill of Rights, but they were opposed to a general statement of first principles in the text of the Constitution. However true, such a statement, by reminding citizens of the right to abolish government, might serve to undermine government, even a government established on those principles. And, as Publius in the Federalist papers, in this instance Alexander Hamilton, insisted, the Constitution was based on those principles: "the Constitution is itself, in every rational sense, and to every useful purpose, A BILL OF RIGHTS" (the federalist #84). It is a bill of natural rights, not because it contains a compendium of those rights but because it is an expression of the natural right of everyone to govern himself and to specify the terms according to which he agrees to give up his natural freedom by submitting to the rules of civil government." The Constitution emanates from us, "THE PEOPLE of the United States," and here in its first sentence, said Publius, "is a better recognition of popular rights than volumes of those aphorisms which make the principal figure in several of our State bills of rights and which would sound much better in a treatise of ethics than in a constitution of government." Natural rights point or lead to government, a government with the power to secure rights, and only secondarily to limitations on governmental power.

In Federalist 84 Hamilton states there were many safeguards against the abuse of power built into the structure of the national government, such as the separation of powers and checks and balances. Hamilton also examines six provisions designed to protect individual liberties. First, to protect the people against executive and judicial abuse of power, the Constitution provides the power to impeach. The President, Vice-President, and all civil officers of the United States, shall be removed from office on impeachment for, and conviction of, treason, bribery, or other high crimes and misdemeanors. Included are all officers of the United States who hold their appointments under the national government, whether their duties are executive or judicial, in the highest or the lowest departments of the government, with the exception of officers of the army and navy. A Senator or Representative of the United States, it was decided, was not a civil officer, within the meaning of this clause in the Constitution. The individual chambers can remove members of the House of Representatives or Senate by way of expulsion if at least two-thirds of the members of the specific chamber vote to do so. Even though the members were elected by the people, no provision for recall by the voters exists.

Second, the writ of habeas corpus (the right that requires that a person arrested must be informed of the charges against them) shall not be suspended, "unless, when in cases of rebellion or invasion the public safety may require it." Habeas corpus is a centuries-old legal procedure that protects against unlawful and indefinite imprisonment. It is a right that is even older than the United States. The practice of unlawful and indefinite imprisonment is a tactic commonly used by tyrannical governments for the purpose of silencing opposition.

Next, Bills of attainder and ex-post-facto laws are prohibited. A bill of attainder is a legislative act that singles out an individual or group for punishment without a trial. An ex post facto law is a law that makes illegal an act that was legal when committed, increases the penalties for an infraction after it has been committed, or changes the rules of evidence to make conviction easier. The great English jurist, Blackstone, believed that prohibiting these types of laws were the two most fundamental individual rights.

Fourth, the Constitution states in Article I, Section 9, Clause 8, "no title of nobility should be granted by the United States." Hamilton writes that the importance of prohibiting titles of nobility is paramount; if such titles were granted, the very foundation of republican government would be undermined. If titles were granted it would also contradict the self-evident truth of the Declaration of Independence that all are born equal.

Fifth, in Article III, Section 2, Clause 3, the Constitution guarantees the right to trial by jury in all criminal cases. This clause takes the ability to convict out of the hands of the government and places it directly with the people in the form of a jury of peers. In our system of law, we also understand that it is the duty of the government to prove guilt and not the duty of the defendant to prove innocence. This is in direct contrast to the system used by tyrants who proclaim guilt and the defendant must prove their innocence, not to a jury of their peers, but to a government appointed panel.

Sixth, treason is very carefully defined in the Constitution in Article III, Section 3 as, "Treason against the United States, shall consist only in levying War against them, or in adhering to their Enemies, giving them Aid and Comfort. No Person shall be convicted of Treason unless on the Testimony of two Witnesses to the same overt Act, or on Confession in open Court."

'The Congress shall have power to declare the Punishment of Treason, but no Attainder of Treason shall work Corruption of Blood, or Forfeiture except during the Life of the Person attainted.'

The Constitution supports the distinction between political dissent and treason, it does all it can to prevent working a hardship on the traitor's family.

Madison states in Federalist 43, "To declare the punishment of treason, but no attainder of treason shall work corruption of blood, or forfeiture, except during the life of the person attained. As treason may be committed against the United States, the authority of the United States ought to be enabled to punish it. But as new-fangled and artificial treasons have been the great engines by which violent factions, the natural offspring of free government, have usually wreaked their alternate malignity on each other, the convention have, with great judgment, opposed a barrier to this peculiar danger, by inserting a constitutional definition of the crime, fixing the proof necessary for conviction of it, and restraining the Congress, even in punishing it, from extending the consequences of guilt beyond the person of its author."

The great achievement of the Constitution, it can safely be said, is the restrictions placed on popular government in favor of the protection of the individual's rights. The Constitution placed the rights of individuals above the needs of the collective thus establishing that the United States was a nation based on the ideal of individualism and not the ideal of collectivism.

RIGHTS IN THE BILL OF RIGHTS

At the Constitutional Convention of 1787, delegates rejected a motion made by George Mason, author of the Virginia Declaration of Rights (1776), to preface the Constitution of the United States with a bill of rights. The failure to mention basic rights soon became a major issue in the subsequent debates over whether the proposed Constitution would be ratified or not.

When the Constitutional Convention ended, delegates went back to their respective states to hold their own ratifying conventions. Each state would decide for itself whether to approve the new framework for the American government or reject it. Article VII of the Constitution stipulated that nine states had to ratify the Constitution for it to go into effect.

The debate over the need for a bill of rights was sparked by a proposal made by a dissenting minority in the Pennsylvania ratifying convention. Some delegates believed that guarantees of certain basic rights and liberties were missing from the proposed Constitution. They called for several amendments that would secure a wide range of liberties, such as the free exercise of religion, freedom of speech and press, and protection against unreasonable searches and seizures. Majorities in the ratifying conventions of New Hampshire, Massachusetts, New York, Maryland, Virginia, North Carolina and South Carolina also called for numerous amendments to the proposed Constitution. Although the substance of these recommended amendments differed from state to state, most contained provisions that would limit the powers of the new federal (national) government and protect the people from inconsistent and oppressive rule.

The Anti-Federalists (those who were opposed to ratifying the Constitution) argued that the broad powers of the new federal government would threaten the powers of the individual states and the liberties of the people. Their major objection to the new Constitution was its lack of a bill of rights. "Bills of rights" list the specific freedoms that governments cannot threaten or take away. When the Constitution was being written, many state constitutions already had bills of rights. For that reason, the authors of the Constitution did not feel it was necessary to have another one. The Anti-Federalists believed that without a list of personal freedoms, the new national government might abuse its powers. They worried that it would destroy the liberties won in the Revolution.

The Anti-Federalists included such patriots as Patrick Henry, the Virginia orator; Sam Adams, the Massachusetts agitator; George Mason, who had written much of the Virginian Constitution; and Richard Henry Lee, who had served as Virginia's delegate to the Continental Congress.

However, the Federalists (those who supported ratification) argued that a bill of rights was unnecessary. Alexander Hamilton, for example, maintained that because the proposed federal government would possess only specifically assigned and limited powers, it could not endanger the fundamental liberties of the people. "Why," he asked, "declare that things shall not be done which there is no power to do? Why, for instance, should it be said that the liberty of the press shall not be restrained, when no power is given by which restrictions may be imposed?" Nevertheless, the

Federalists had to pledge their support for the addition of a bill of rights to the Constitution once the new government began operations. Otherwise they would risk endangering the Constitution's ratification in certain key states and face the possibility of another constitutional convention.

James Madison, the "Father of the Constitution," may also be considered the "Father of the Bill of Rights." In his campaign for a seat in the House of Representatives under the new Constitution, he promised his voters in Virginia that he would energetically push for the adoption of a bill of rights. True to his word, he took the lead in the First Congress in pressing for the desired amendments.

On June 8, 1789, drawing from proposals made by the various state ratifying conventions, Madison proposed to the Congress nine amendments to the Constitution, containing nineteen specific provisions (many of which are now contained in the Bill of Rights). Madison and members of a House committee then went through the complex process of drafting a bill that would secure the necessary two-thirds approval of both houses of Congress. The House and the Senate modified some of Madison's proposals, eliminated others entirely, and added some new ones as well.

As it finally emerged from Congress, the proposed Bill of Rights consisted of twelve amendments and was offered to the states for ratification. The first two proposed amendments were never ratified by the states. (One was related to the size of the House of Representatives and the other was regarding the compensation, or payment, for senators and representatives.) On December 15, 1791, Virginia ratified the remaining ten amendments, and the Bill of Rights officially became part of the Constitution.

The 10 Amendments and What They Protect

The First Amendment: Basic Liberties

The First Amendment is perhaps the most important part of the Bill of Rights. It protects five of the most basic liberties. They are freedom of religion, freedom of speech, freedom of the press, freedom of assembly, and freedom to petition the government to right wrongs. These were the guarantees that the Anti-Federalists missed most in the new Constitution.

Freedom of Religion, like so many rights, is misunderstood. The Amendment reads that "Congress shall make no law respecting an establishment of religion or prohibiting the free exercise thereof." Congress cannot establish a national religion nor can congress prohibit any person from practicing their religion. Many of the colonies had official state sponsored religions. For instance, Virginia, New York, Maryland, North Carolina, and South Carolina had the Church of England as their state sponsored Church. Massachusetts, Connecticut, and New Hampshire had the Congregational Church as their state sponsored Church. The Bill of Rights said the United States government could not establish a state sponsored Church and could not restrict the free practice of religion, even in public. Freedom of religion is the protection of the right to pray and or worship without restriction as to where one might pray or worship including a public building. It is critical to remember that freedom of religion is the protection of and not freedom from religion.

Freedom of Speech protects our right to think what we like and say what we please even if the speech or thought might be deemed to be hateful or offensive. If we the people are to govern ourselves, we must have these rights, even if they are abused by a minority. Congress is to make no law to abridge or restrict this freedom. This freedom is critical to a free society. It is one of the very first rights to be restricted under a totalitarian state. Freedom of speech and thought encourages nonconformity within a society. Totalitarian states require conformity of thought, word, and deed and punish those who would speak and think freely. Our founders understood how critical freedom of speech is.

"If freedom of speech is taken away, then dumb and silent we may be led, like sheep to the slaughter." George Washington

"Whoever would overthrow the liberty of a nation must begin by subduing the freeness of speech." Benjamin Franklin

The founders viewed freedom of speech as a part of the overall natural right to liberty and that it is the fundamental job of government to secure this natural right as it is the fundamental job of government to secure all-natural rights.

Freedom of the Press. This freedom is supposed to keep citizens informed about what is happening in government. It helps the people to be informed and thus be responsible citizens. The press is free to criticize the government without the risk of punishment or censorship. News reports do not have to be submitted for government inspection before they are published. This censorship would violate the First Amendment.

It was recognized by our founders, they were often the recipient, that the press was often not accurate, fair, or even truthful. They understood however, that censorship in any form was always a greater danger to freedom. Thomas Jefferson expressed this very thought in his second inaugural address when he stated, "Since truth and reason have maintained their ground against false opinions in league with false facts, the press confined to truth needs no other legal restraint. The public judgment will correct false reasonings and opinions on a full hearing of all parties, and no other definite line can be drawn between the inestimable liberty of the press and its demoralizing licentiousness. If there be still improprieties which this rule would not restrain, its supplement must be sought in the censorship of public opinion."

Freedom of Assembly. This freedom makes it possible for Americans to join groups or political organizations even if those groups or political organizations represent unpopular views. Because of the right to assemble freely, people can join groups or political organizations that oppose the popular beliefs of the day. Freedom of Assembly is a direct form of Freedom of Speech. The right to assemble peaceably and express an opposing or a consenting view cannot be limited or punished.

Freedom to Petition. This important freedom allows people to tell the government what they think is needed. They can try to prevent the government from acting in a certain way. They can complain to the government without fear of penalty when things aren't going the way they should. For example, if people dump garbage near your school, you can petition the government to clean it. Freedom to petition can also let the government know how well it is doing its job.

The Second Amendment: The Right to Bear Arms

The Second Amendment guarantees individual states the right to maintain "a well-regulated militia," and citizens the right to "keep and bear arms." We must always remember why this amendment was made a part of the Bill of Rights. It was not so the citizen could buy a gun for hunting, for recreational purposes, or for self-protection. The purpose was for the people to be able to protect their freedom from those who would take it from them; an oppressive government.

"Before a standing army can rule, the people must be disarmed; as they are in almost every kingdom of Europe. The supreme power in America cannot enforce unjust laws by the sword; because the whole body of the people are armed and constitute a force superior to any band of regular troops that can be, on any pretense, raised in the United States." Noah Webster

The Third Amendment: Housing Troops

The Third Amendment pledges that in peacetime, citizens will never have to keep soldiers in their homes without consenting. Before the Revolution, the British forced Americans to provide lodging and food for their troops. The colonists bitterly resented this intrusion on their privacy as well as the cost of feeding hungry soldiers. It would be great to know that this intrusion could never happen again.

The Fourth Amendment: Searchers and Seizure

The Fourth through Eighth Amendments concern the rights of people suspected of crime. The Fourth Amendment protects citizens from improper searches of their bodies, possessions, or homes. It requires that a detailed warrant be issued by a judge listing what can be searched. There must be a good reason for the search. The government cannot search just because you are of a different political persuasion with the hopes of finding something so they could then charge you with a crime.

The Fifth Amendment: Rights of the Accused, Due Process of the Law, and Eminent Domain

Rights of the Accused. The Fifth Amendment protects the rights of anyone accused of a crime. The common phrase is that a person is innocent until proven guilty. This is a misleading phrase since a person who has committed a crime is guilty and one who has not committed a crime is innocent. Proof in a court of law does not determine actual guilt or innocence, but only guilt or innocence for legal purposes.

The significance of the amendment is where the burden of proof lies. Because of this amendment, the burden of proof lies with the government or the accuser. The defendant has no obligation to even present a defense. This is different from what we find in totalitarian states where if the government charges an individual with a crime, the defendant must then prove their innocence. The government or accuser does not have to present a case.

The Fifth Amendment also states that the person cannot be tried twice for the same crime.

The section of the Fifth Amendment that has received the most publicity is the guarantee against "self-incrimination." This means people cannot be forced to testify against themselves. Under the Fifth Amendment, law enforcement officials must produce the evidence necessary to convict a person of a crime. The accused person cannot be made to provide it. In some societies people are tortured until they confessed to crimes they may or may not have committed.

Due Process of the Law is another section of the Fifth Amendment that holds that "no one can be deprived of life, liberty, or property without due process of law." The government must follow certain legal procedures before deciding on a penalty. It can't jail a person because it suspects that the person committed a crime. It must prove the accusation by following certain rules and methods. However, "due process of law" is a rather vague and general term so consequently it is not applied the same in all cases.

Eminent Domain. The Fifth Amendment requires the government pay citizens when it confiscates their property for a public use. The government's right to take this property is called "eminent domain." Suppose the state wanted to build a highway which would run right through your residence. The state would have to pay you a reasonable price for the property. The government could force you to move, but at least it would have to have paid you supposedly the same value you would have received in an uncoerced or a market-based transaction.

The Sixth Amendment: Fair and Speedy Trials

The Sixth Amendment provides more requirements for a fair trial in criminal cases. It guarantees a speedy, public trial by an impartial jury in the area where the crime was committed. The defendant must be able to question the accusers and to force favorable witnesses to testify. The accused has a right to a lawyer.

The Seventh Amendment: Jury Trials

The Seventh Amendment guarantees that Americans will receive a jury trial in civil (as opposed to criminal cases because that right is protected in the body of the Constitution) cases involving property worth more than $20. Today, however, people do not bring such cases to federal courts unless a much larger sum of money is involved.

The Eighth Amendment: Bails, Fines, and Punishments

The Eighth Amendment protects people from having to pay unreasonably high "bail" in order to be released from jail before they go to trial. Bail is money given to pledge that a person accused of a crime will appear for trial. The Eighth Amendment also protects people from unreasonably high fines. Finally, the amendment outlaws cruel and unusual punishment. This requirement, as well as the Fifth Amendment's guarantee against self-incrimination, protects citizens from the use of torture.

The Ninth and Tenth Amendments: Reserved Powers

The last two amendments address the liberties of citizens and the rights of states. The Ninth Amendment states that the Constitution and the Bill of Rights do not define all the fundamental rights people have. Such rights exist whether or not they are defined or listed.

The Tenth Amendment makes a similar claim concerning the rights of the states and people. It holds that the states and the people have powers that are set aside and not listed item by item. These powers are called "reserved powers." They can be contrasted with "express powers," which are specifically defined in the Constitution.

These two amendments clearly state the intent that our government was to be a limited government. If it was the intent of the founders that we were to have an unlimited government and the rights of the people and the states were to be limited, these amendments would read exactly the opposite stating that rights not listed were therefore under the province of the government and the power and rights of government would be unlimited. This intent is made even more clear with Jefferson expressing how important this limitation of government is.

"The Tenth Amendment is the foundation of the Constitution." - Thomas Jefferson

A RIGHT OR AN ENTITLEMENT

In his first treatise, John Locke explicitly refuted the idea that kings rule according to divine right (from God) and argued that human beings have natural rights upon which the government may not infringe. This view of government was a radical view. The common view was that government determined the rights of the people and was not that government is morally obliged to serve people, namely by protecting life, liberty, and property.

Many today argue that people have "rights" to education, jobs, health care, housing, income, and so many more. At the same time these same people argue that government has the right to define and limit the natural rights as defined by Locke; the right of every individual to life, liberty, and property. Americans, no, perhaps all people, have become confused. All people must understand what a right is, what an entitlement is, and is an entitlement ever a right.

Rights do not include money, material items, or services. Therefore, rights never require forcibly taking from others or authorizing the government to perform this confiscation for you. The only role government plays regarding rights is to protect those rights, ensuring that the individual retains their right to life, liberty, and property and that the individual does not have these rights infringed by others or by government.

The United States Senate Glossary defines entitlement as: A Federal program or provision of law that requires payments to any person or unit of government that meets the eligibility criteria established by law. Entitlements constitute a binding obligation on the part of the Federal Government, and eligible recipients have legal recourse if the obligation is not fulfilled.

The Oxford dictionary defines a "right" as "a moral or legal entitlement to have or do something."

The same book defines an "entitlement" as "a government scheme that provides benefits to any individual meeting certain eligibility requirements."

A right does not include government. An individual exercising their right does not require a contribution in any form from another person. The individual has the same right if they are the only person or if they are one among many.

An entitlement can never be granted to a person without the aid of an institution, generally government, and another person who must have less so the other can receive the "entitlement."

In the United States, over time, as we have indicated, certain factions would have us belief that right and entitlement mean the same. These same people would have us believe there is no separation between these two words. The same faction that wants to morph together these two words also would have us believe that our natural rights come from government and are not endowed to each individual by the Creator. Yes, this same faction would also have us believe that entitlements are natural rights.

For our Republic to remain free and independent, or perhaps regain our freedom and independence, it is imperative that we understand and accept that the rights defined in the Declaration of

Independence, The Constitution of the United States, and The Bill of Rights are natural rights endowed by our Creator. The purpose of the Bill of Rights was to ensure that those natural rights, not entitlements, are not violated by the government that we, the people, created and are allowing to govern us, not control or enslave us.

It is critical for our freedom and independence that we understand the role of government is not the giver of natural rights but the protector of our natural rights. Since the government did not grant the natural right it cannot take the right from us nor limit that right. It is supposed to only protect that right so that the right is not diminished by government or by others.

An entitlement is something controlled by government because it came into existence through a law or a program allowing the government to provide those services or benefits to those individuals who meet the stated requirements. The government can provide these entitlements only by taking from fellow citizens, so the government has the means to provide the entitlement. Entitlements are essential to a collectivist (Marxist, communist, socialist, progressive, Democrat – all virtually the same) controlled government. They gain their legitimacy by deceiving the public into accepting that rights and entitlements are the same. During the ongoing health care debate, collectivists said that healthcare was a right. They are correct that individuals have a right to seek healthcare, but it is not a right that healthcare will be provided to individuals by taking from others to provide it. It has been stated that if free healthcare was a right, then doctors would be required to give that service to individuals for free. That would be a condition which would put those doctors into servitude, or slavery. But then that is what the collectivist does believe; that the individual is a slave to the state, and it is the purpose of the individual to subordinate everything to the state to redistribute based on some perceived needs basis.

What then are individual natural rights? Imagine you were living in a world with no borders, governments, or any type of restriction; a right is anything you could do that didn't affect others.

You could say you had the right to do whatever you wanted.

You could say whatever you wanted.

You could think whatever you wanted.

You could worship whoever, whenever, and however you wanted.

You could carry whatever you needed to defend yourself.

No one would be able to take what is yours or enter your dwelling.

You could print anything you wanted.

You could meet anyone and gather in large groups.

You would not have to buy anything you did not want.

In the same scenario as described above, unless someone else was willing to give the following things to you through their own generosity:

You would have to find a way to earn your own income.

You would have to pay for your own healthcare.

You would have to gather your own food or work for it.

You would have to build your own house or find one that you could afford.

You would have to pay your own tuition or find a free educator.

If any of this latter list was received by you because you met certain eligibility requirements of some program, and another had to have less so you could have the above, it is an entitlement.

When anybody states, "it's my right," it is not your right if government is involved through a law or a program and they have to take from another to pay for what you or a collectivist (Marxist, communist, socialist, progressive, Democrat – all virtually the same) say is your right. If government was involved through a redistribution scheme of any sort, it's an entitlement and it's not a right.

TWO VISIONS OF AMERICA

There are 'Two Visions of America". One vision is a vision believing that we are a nation that believes we have natural rights given to us by our Creator that are independent of government and are not granted to us because another has sacrificed for us willingly or unwillingly. The other vision believes that it is the duty and right of government to control the lives of the citizen, that government has the duty and the right to dictate to individuals how they are to live their lives, even how they are to think. As a function of controlling the individual, in this vision, government decides who should have what and how much they should have. In this vision there is no difference between a right and an entitlement, because government has total control over everything, yes even the lives and the thoughts of the individual.

In the previous chapters of this book, we have discussed natural rights, how our national documents, the Declaration of Independence, the Constitution of the United States, and the Bill of Rights regarded natural rights. We have explored the concepts of entitlements being regarded as rights.

The vision of the one America is a vision about a unique people who determined they would be a people who separated what they declared to be natural rights and were the province of The Creator and not the province of government, from the control of government. The vision of the other America, the one which declares all rights are the province of government and does not distinguish between natural rights and entitlements, determines that it is the role of government to control all including the lives and thoughts of the individual.

Once upon a time, years and years ago, there was a land with many different states. Each of these states had a government and at the head of that government was an individual who told the people that he was the direct representative of God on earth and the head of the government because God willed it. The people accepted this as truth and believed that this head of government, as a direct representative of God, was in total control of their rights of life, liberty, and property or lack thereof. The people believed that the representative of God could determine who lived and who died, what liberty everyone had or did not have, and who could or could not own property.

In these lands, years ago, the direct representative could and did declare that certain individuals and certain classes of people could be executed, murdered, or have their life ended simply because it was declared that the individual would be or was an inconvenience to another. The life of the human was thought to be no more valuable, and in many instances, not as valuable as an animal or even an insect. The representative or government told the people that if an animal becomes a nuisance and is more trouble than they are worth, just murder it, if an insect is an inconvenience just kill it, and if an individual such as an unborn child was going to cause a drastic unwanted life change or cause other sorts of inconveniences, just eliminate the perceived cause of the inconvenience. It was believed and practiced that because the representative of God was the government, government had the right to declare life of the human to be of no more value than that of an animal or insect and was thus just as dispensable.

The liberties of an individual were also determined by the representative of government. It was the right of the representative or government to dictate to the individual how that individual would live their life. The wishes or desires of the individual were unimportant. If an individual found a new and innovative way to produce a greater yield of whatever product they produced, the representative or government determined the benefits of the innovation belonged to government, because without the government the innovation could never have happened. It was the government who determined your vocation and that vocation would depend upon the status of your family, along with your class at birth, and what the government determined they needed at the time. The more compliant and conforming the individual was to the demands of the government, the more favorably they would be viewed.

Basic liberties were dictated by the government as well. If the individual disagreed with government, they were punished if they openly voiced that disagreement. Remember, the representative of government was placed in their position by divine providence and could never be wrong. The individual was always expected to say only what was approved by the government. The individual was punished for statements deemed to be provocative, insulting, hateful, or not in conformity with the policies of government. Criticism of the representative was never allowed. There were dire consequences for those considered to be repetitive violators of this non-conforming speech or speech that was deemed to be inappropriate or hateful.

How you worshiped God or if you could worship God, was dictated by the government. What, if any, worship that was allowed was determined by the representative or government at any time. In most of the states only one form of worship was allowed. Anybody caught, or in some cases even suspected of worshiping in any non-conforming manner, could be severely punished even to the point of death. There were certainly no public signs of another belief from that demanded by government nor were their public displays of what we might term as non-conforming beliefs. Worship was not considered to be an individual choice but was instead an exercise that was dictated by government.

Censorship was right and proper according to government. Anything, written or spoken that did not conform to the ideals of the government, was determined to be detrimental to the good of the country. Education was not allowed. Education institutions were instead indoctrination institutions. It was the purpose of these institutions to teach only what was approved by and believed by government. Anything that did not conform to the standards dictated by government was heresy and not allowed to be discussed, much less taught.

All groups were monitored. No group of greater than three could meet unless the group was approved by the government, and even if the group was approved there could be no gathering unless a government official was present. Spontaneous group meetings would be dealt with harshly, resulting in serious injury and even death to many who were intentionally in the group or were just in the wrong place at the wrong time. No group could gather if the government even suspected malicious intent and was quickly disbanded if the government representative reported malicious intent, even if none had been present.

The government had the right to search the dwelling or the contents of an individual for any reason and at any time. Many times, the only reason for a search was to inconvenience or harass the inhabitant because the government or representative disliked or distrusted the inhabitant, thought it would be fun, or simply had nothing better to do.

If the government decided to arrest an individual, nothing more was needed by the government than the desire to arrest based on a desire or possibly a suspicion, warranted or not. The government could leave you in a prison cell for as long as they desired without ever making a formal charge. If the government unilaterally determined to bring you before a court and hold a trial, that trial may or may not be before a jury, and if it was before a jury, it would be a jury selected and approved by the government. The government would make the charge and then it would be the responsibility of the arrested individual to prove they did not commit the crime the government charged. The individual was presumed to be guilty and must prove their innocence.

In those times, years and years ago, the government was never wrong, was all powerful, and all rights of the individual were denied or granted at the behest of the government with no appeal available to the individual. The government was lord over everything and controller of the lives and the thoughts of the individual. The individual was a slave to the government. The government considered themselves to be the grantor of all making the individual totally dependent on the goodness, generosity, or benevolence of the divine representative.

After many promises and many delays, finally, one of these government representatives agreed to allow a group of people, a group who had been asking for several years if they could take a boat ride toward where the sun set to learn what was there, to take that ride. These adventurous people discovered a new land, a land that was not divided into states nor did it have formal governments with representatives who believed they were placed at the head of the government by God. This new place was unlike anything known at the time. Other government representatives from other states heard about this new land and they sent their people to learn more about this strange place as well.

Eventually, more and more people began to come to this new land. The people who came, came for many different reasons. Some came because they were non-conformists who did not fit well with society. Others came because they resented government dictating who and how they could worship God. Others came because they refused to have government tell them how they were to live their lives and what they were to think or say. Others were sent there by government because government no longer wanted the expense of keeping these actual criminals or jailed non-conformists in prison. Yet others were shipped to this new land because they were simply deemed to be non-desirables. Some went to this new land because they were ambitious individuals who wanted to be away from the confines and dictates of government and because they believed they had the abilities, drive, desire, and fortitude, that if left alone, they could become successful beyond their wildest dreams.

It was indeed a strange conglomeration of people who reached the shores of the new land. The one common trait this strange conglomeration of people had was that they desired to be free from the restraints and constraints of government. These individuals did not expect anything from government, and they did not want anything from government. They had the intuition that when an individual was given something by government, government would expect something in return. This to a large part was the source of their non-conformity. These people also intuitively knew that government was nothing more than a conglomeration of people, just as they were, and those in government were not the source of rights.

As we move forward in time, we learn that this varied group of people become more and more independent, rejecting the ideas that birth, government, or any source other than themselves had any right to determine the course of their lives. They more and more became individuals who learned that they were responsible for the choices they made, and for the consequences of those choices, be they good or be they bad. These independent people, a people who were a long way from the government that ruled them, began to understand they had rights; rights to life, liberty, and property, and these rights were independent of government.

That far away government realized that these people were becoming to independent and because of that growing independence had concluded that the price of depending on government always came with a high cost to their freedom, a cost these people determined they were no longer willing to pay. In response to this newfound disdain for government authority, the government began to exercise more and more control, telling these people how they were to live their lives and what their thoughts were to be.

The inevitable clash between those who believed government should have a minimal role on the lives of the citizens, a role that should be limited to that of a protector, and those who believed the role of government was to be sovereign with the people serving that government, eventually happened. The result of the clash was that this conglomeration of misfits and non-conformists won the clash and became free from the constraints of that government that had determined it was the role of government to dictate to the people what course their lives should take and what thoughts they should have, a government that believed it was the proper role of government to determine what rights the citizens could have.

This group of people, now independent from the constraints of what they considered to be tyranny, set about the onerous task of forming a nation. In the formation of that nation, these people did understand that they would have to form a government. They also understood that any government they would form, it would be that government that would be the single biggest threat to the freedoms they had just won.

In order to protect those freedoms from the tyranny of government these people formed a government unlike anything ever seen before. These unique people understood that all their rights came from their Creator and that government had no role in connection with these rights other than to be the protector of these rights.

These people said that since life was a gift from the Creator to each individual, government did not have any right to determine who would live or who would not. This applied to individuals or to classes of people; classes such as the unborn for instance. The only exception to this role of government over the natural right of life was when it was determined that an individual took the life of another, thus depriving another person of their natural right of life.

These people also determined that those rights so fundamental to liberty were not to be infringed upon by government. In this new land with this new concept of limited government, government would have no right to determine what people could or could not say. The people understood, that some people could and would say some harmful and insulting things that would hurt feelings and cause pain. They also understood that once exceptions were made to this essential liberty of freedom, the natural propensity of those who serve in government would be to limit even more this fundamental liberty of speech. This would be surrendering a natural right to those in government who would then have more and more control over the lives of the people.

In addition to free speech, these people forming this new government understood that curtailments on the other essential liberties to freedom, those including but not limited to religion, the press, assembly, the right to petition the government without fear of being reprimanded, and the right to bear arms to protect these freedoms from the inevitable abuses of government were essential.

Understanding that government will always attempt to gain control over the lives and thoughts of the people, those forming this new government added even more safeguards to protect their freedom. This newly formed government would not be allowed to arrest people just because people opposed the government. The government would have to have cause for arrests and would have to fulfill certain requirements. These requirements were designed to limit the power of government. The critical safeguard was that in this new nation, the burden of proving guilt would always be the burden of the government or prosecutor. This was an essential rule of freedom. A defendant or the accused had no responsibility to prove their innocence even to the point of not even being required to present a defense if they so choose.

The liberties of the people were never to be infringed upon by government because these liberties were endowed by the Creator and were out of the control or regulation of the government. These people understood that this principle was essential to this new nation if they were to remain free from the tyrannical rule of government.

Along with life and liberty, the people understood that the right to property was also given by the Creator and not the government. People owned property and were free from the government confiscating their property or dictating that the property be used for the benefit of the government and not the benefit of the owner. More importantly perhaps, the people understood that property rights extended beyond the rights to land or buildings but extended to the person. Property of an individual included their talents, their earning capacity, their desires, and their ambitions. The government had no power to tell an individual what vocation they must pursue or which talents they must develop. The people were free to pursue their own happiness, in fact were encouraged to do so. In this new state, an individual was not relegated or elevated to certain positions because of their position at birth based on factors such as into which family or class they were born. All were free to determine their own course in life, dictated only by talents, ambition, and temperament.

This new state and the people of this new state were indeed unique. The world had never seen such individualists, non-conformists, and independent people who believed the function of government was to serve the people as opposed to the people serving a sovereign government, adhering to government dictates, and depending on government to provide their needs as government determined their needs to be.

These individualists, non-conformists, and independents began a story the likes of which the world had never known. They became adventurers, innovators, competitors, people who failed but refused to accept defeat and started over, protectors of others, good neighbors, good families, and loyal patriots to the country who understood governments function was to serve and protect the people from foreign enemies and invaders. These people understood they were the envy of the world because their rights of life, liberty, and property came from their Creator and not from government. They also understood entitlements were a government means to gain sovereignty and place the people in a state of enslavement. These people understood entitlements were a means of regressing to those days long ago when government believed it was the grantor and controller of the people's rights.

Overtime the fabric of the state built by individualists, non-conformists, and independent people began to change. As the country became the most powerful state in the world, economically and militarily, some of the people began to believe that others who achieved and excelled must share the benefits of their talents and efforts with the less ambitious. These people began to profess that government must control and restrict the rights endowed by the Creator to the people. After several years, many of these people openly claimed that it was the role of government to regulate all the natural rights because these natural rights, without control and regulation, would bring about what they considered to be, unfair results or inequality. A method of the government regulating and bringing about what they considered to be more fair results or equality, would be accomplished by instituting entitlements.

As generally happens the use of entitlements began gradually. The amounts of wealth the government confiscated to share with others as a part of the entitlement program mentality was small. The entitlements were small, the number who received the entitlements was small, and the length of time they were received was short. Over time all of this changed. Those in government who supported these entitlements soon began to learn that the recipients of the entitlements became dependent on them and consequently became a very loyal voting bloc to all who would promise and promote these entitlements. When those in government who supported entitlements learned of the power they gained as they increased the amount confiscated so the amount of the entitlement could be increased, as well as the length of time it could be paid, others in government believed this was truly the way to gain and to keep power.

The idea of some that confiscating, through government programs, more and more of the hard-earned rewards of the producers created a divide within the state. The power-hungry government officials became aware of this divide, so to combat any backlash against them for literally creating a government dependent class of people who willing received the confiscated assets of their fellow citizens, these power hungry government officials began to tell the people that natural rights are entitlements given by the government and entitlements are human rights deserved by all.

These power-hungry government officials, who now begin to actually believe natural rights were granted and therefore should be controlled by government. said things such as who could live or die was up to the government, and who could be born should be called a choice and not murder. These power-hungry government officials said that it was up to the government to determine what liberties people would have; speech was not free speech if it offended somebody, assembly could not take place if it was determined to be discriminatory, and the government could only be petitioned if the resulting action would bring about what was determined to be politically incorrect.

Equal rights were also redefined to mean that the rights of any person who was determined to be a minority and therefore was somehow a victim would have to have greater rights, so in the politically correct mind the rights would now be equal. It was also determined that to reinforce this new definition of equal rights, the government would have to be placed in the position to determine, on a case by case basis, where the burden of proof would lie; with the accuser or the accused. In cases where a politically correct victim was the accuser, it was determined the burden of proof would lie with the accused. If the accused was a politically correct victim, the burden of proof would lie with the accuser. These power-hungry people explained that the politically correct position is more important to society than the protection of the burden of proof principle as stated by those who founded this new state.

There are now two visions being told in one state. One of the visions is the vision based on the individualist, non-conforming, and independent person who believed that their rights were given to them by their Creator and the only role government would play in this scenario would be to protect those rights. In this vision the people believe they must be allowed to make their own decisions. They also understand that the consequences of their decisions are their responsibility, good or bad. These people understand that the role of government must be very limited, never picking winners or losers, never punishing the achiever, always respecting the rights of life, liberty, and property given to each individual by the Creator, and always understanding that government cannot be a charity or a slave master with its citizens dependent on government for their economic survival.

Vision number two is exactly the opposite. In vision number two, government becomes the controller and protector of all. It is accepted that the rights of life, liberty, and property are not truly rights but gifts of government to be given and withdrawn for any purpose government officials believe to be in the best interest of the collective, group, or state. In this vision it is believed that the role of government is to bring about a conforming and subservient society that is totally equal, socially and economically. It is believed that a major role of government is to be the primary receiver of all national income so the proceeds can be spread in any way government determines is in the best interest of the collective, group, or state.

The ending of each vision is already known because the visions have been seen before; vision one a few times and vison two, many times. Vision one ends with a vibrant nation both economically and militarily. The people are a dynamic, innovative, and responsible people who are builders and creators. Poverty does exist in this society but only because poverty is relative. The standard of living for all is extremely high with all but a very few not having conveniences and luxuries. Those considered to be living in poverty, have essentials, and even some luxuries, compared to those living in real poverty in other areas of the world.

The ending of vision two is also known. Every time vision two is told, it ends in a state where society is in a state of social collapse, financial collapse, it becomes a society of despair, a society of devestation, and a society where all hope is gone. Poverty abounds everywhere. There is no middle class. Food, water, clothing, and other necessities are rare, if available at all. Since poverty is relative, those who advocated for the policies that created this devastated society, argue there is no poverty because there is equality. The only people who have conveniences and luxuries are the few who are in power and they claim this is just because they are sacrificing their time for the good of the people.

Nations and societies are always in some state of vision number one or vision number two. Those power-hungry government officials who advocate for vision number two always have the same story; government should be in control of natural rights, entitlements are the rights of the so-called victims, and the individual is not responsible for the consequences of their actions – society is. These power-hungry government officials explain that their version of vision number two will somehow end differently, even though the policies they advocate are the same as those advocated in every version of vision number two.

Vision number one is more difficult for people because it requires people to be responsible for the consequences of their actions, be they good or be they bad. It requires that people respect the hard work, talents, and determination of others and not covet the rewards of the efforts of others. These people quickly learn that to covet, is a needless endeavor, because they can accomplish whatever they wish regardless of what somebody else has achieved. These people understand that these good things such as happiness, achievement, rewards, and satisfaction are not finite, but they are infinite, limited only by the desire, talents, and efforts of the individual. The rewards are not because of the family or class into which the individual was born. They are not because of the class of victimhood to which some power-hungry government official wishes to place the individual.

The rewards are the result of the individual understanding their right to life, liberty, property or pursuit of happiness is a right the Creator has endowed upon them and the results, good or bad, are because of the choices and efforts of the individual.

No matter what power-hungry government officials say or wish us to believe, natural rights are endowed to each person by the Creator and not by man nor government. Entitlements are not rights. Entitlements are given by power-hungry government officials who understand that entitlements are the means to their own power and wealth while enslaving the people. For entitlements to exist, government must exist, and government must confiscate from one to gift to another.

FOUNDING DOCUMENTS

THE DECLARATION OF INDEPENENCE

IN CONGRESS, JULY 4, 1776

The unanimous Declaration of the thirteen united States of America

When in the Course of human events it becomes necessary for one people to dissolve the political bands which have connected them with another and to assume among the powers of the earth, the separate and equal station to which the Laws of Nature and of Nature's God entitle them, a decent respect to the opinions of mankind requires that they should declare the causes which impel them to the separation.

We hold these truths to be self-evident, that all men are created equal, that they are endowed by their Creator with certain unalienable Rights, that among these are Life, Liberty and the pursuit of

Happiness. — That to secure these rights, Governments are instituted among Men, deriving their just powers from the consent of the governed, — That whenever any Form of Government becomes destructive of these ends, it is the Right of the People to alter or to abolish it, and to institute new Government, laying its foundation on such principles and organizing its powers in such form, as to them shall seem most likely to effect their Safety and Happiness. Prudence, indeed, will dictate that Governments long established should not be changed for light and transient causes; and accordingly all experience hath shewn that mankind are more disposed to suffer, while evils are sufferable than to right themselves by abolishing the forms to which they are accustomed. But when a long train of abuses and usurpations, pursuing invariably the same Object evinces a design to reduce them under absolute Despotism, it is their right, it is their duty, to throw off such Government, and to provide new Guards for their future security. — Such has been the patient sufferance of these Colonies; and such is now the necessity which constrains them to alter their former Systems of

Government. The history of the present King of Great Britain is a history of repeated injuries and usurpations, all having in direct object the establishment of an absolute Tyranny over these States. To prove this, let Facts be submitted to a candid world.

He has refused his Assent to Laws, the most wholesome and necessary for the public good.

He has forbidden his Governors to pass Laws of immediate and pressing importance, unless suspended in their operation till his Assent should be obtained; and when so suspended, he has utterly neglected to attend to them.

He has refused to pass other Laws for the accommodation of large districts of people, unless those people would relinquish the right of Representation in the Legislature, a right inestimable to them and formidable to tyrants only.

He has called together legislative bodies at places unusual, uncomfortable, and distant from the depository of their Public Records, for the sole purpose of fatiguing them into compliance with his measures.

He has dissolved Representative Houses repeatedly, for opposing with manly firmness his invasions on the rights of the people.

He has refused for a long time, after such dissolutions, to cause others to be elected, whereby the Legislative Powers, incapable of Annihilation, have returned to the People at large for their exercise; the State remaining in the mean time exposed to all the dangers of invasion from without, and convulsions within.

He has endeavored to prevent the population of these States; for that purpose obstructing the Laws for Naturalization of Foreigners; refusing to pass others to encourage their migrations hither, and raising the conditions of new Appropriations of Lands.

He has obstructed the Administration of Justice by refusing his Assent to Laws for establishing Judiciary Powers.

He has made Judges dependent on his Will alone for the tenure of their offices, and the amount and payment of their salaries.

He has erected a multitude of New Offices, and sent hither swarms of Officers to harass our people and eat out their substance.

He has kept among us, in times of peace, Standing Armies without the Consent of our legislatures.

He has affected to render the Military independent of and superior to the Civil Power.

He has combined with others to subject us to a jurisdiction foreign to our constitution, and unacknowledged by our laws; giving his Assent to their Acts of pretended Legislation:

For quartering large bodies of armed troops among us:

For protecting them, by a mock Trial from punishment for any Murders which they should commit on the Inhabitants of these States:

For cutting off our Trade with all parts of the world:

For imposing Taxes on us without our Consent:

For depriving us in many cases, of the benefit of Trial by Jury:

For transporting us beyond Seas to be tried for pretended offences:

For abolishing the free System of English Laws in a neighbouring Province, establishing therein an Arbitrary government, and enlarging its Boundaries so as to render it at once an example and fit instrument for introducing the same absolute rule into these Colonies

For taking away our Charters, abolishing our most valuable Laws and altering fundamentally the Forms of our Governments:

For suspending our own Legislatures, and declaring themselves invested with power to legislate for us in all cases whatsoever.

He has abdicated Government here, by declaring us out of his Protection and waging War against us.

He has plundered our seas, ravaged our coasts, burnt our towns, and destroyed the lives of our people.

He is at this time transporting large Armies of foreign Mercenaries to compleat the works of death, desolation, and tyranny, already begun with circumstances of Cruelty & Perfidy scarcely paralleled in the most barbarous ages, and totally unworthy the Head of a civilized nation.

He has constrained our fellow Citizens taken Captive on the high Seas to bear Arms against their Country, to become the executioners of their friends and Brethren, or to fall themselves by their Hands.

He has excited domestic insurrections amongst us, and has endeavoured to bring on the inhabitants of our frontiers, the merciless Indian Savages whose known rule of warfare, is an undistinguished destruction of all ages, sexes and conditions.

In every stage of these Oppressions We have Petitioned for Redress in the most humble terms: Our repeated Petitions have been answered only by repeated injury. A Prince, whose character is thus marked by every act which may define a Tyrant, is unfit to be the ruler of a free people.

Nor have We been wanting in attentions to our British brethren. We have warned them from time to time of attempts by their legislature to extend an unwarrantable jurisdiction over us. We have reminded them of the circumstances of our emigration and settlement here. We have appealed to their native justice and magnanimity, and we have conjured them by the ties of our common kindred to disavow these usurpations, which would inevitably interrupt our connections and correspondence. They too have been deaf to the voice of justice and of consanguinity. We must, therefore, acquiesce in the necessity, which denounces our Separation, and hold them, as we hold the rest of mankind, Enemies in War, in Peace Friends.

We, therefore, the Representatives of the united States of America, in General Congress, Assembled, appealing to the Supreme Judge of the world for the rectitude of our intentions, do, in the Name, and by Authority of the good People of these Colonies, solemnly publish and declare, That these united Colonies are, and of Right ought to be Free and Independent States, that they are Absolved from all Allegiance to the British Crown, and that all political connection between them and the State of Great Britain, is and ought to be totally dissolved; and that as Free and Independent States, they have full Power to levy War, conclude Peace, contract Alliances, establish Commerce, and to do all other Acts and Things which Independent States may of right do. — And for the support of this Declaration, with a firm reliance on the protection of Divine Providence, we mutually pledge to each other our Lives, our Fortunes, and our sacred Honor.

THE CONSTITUTION OF THE UNITED STATES

We the People of the United States, in Order to form a more perfect Union, establish Justice, insure domestic Tranquility, provide for the common defence, promote the general Welfare, and secure the Blessings of Liberty to ourselves and our Posterity, do ordain and establish this Constitution for the United States of America.

Article I (Article 1 - Legislative)

Section 1

All legislative Powers herein granted shall be vested in a Congress of the United States, which shall consist of a Senate and House of Representatives.

Section 2

1: The House of Representatives shall be composed of Members chosen every second Year by the People of the several States, and the Electors in each State shall have the Qualifications requisite for Electors of the most numerous Branch of the State Legislature.

2: No Person shall be a Representative who shall not have attained to the Age of twenty five Years, and been seven Years a Citizen of the United States, and who shall not, when elected, be an Inhabitant of that State in which he shall be chosen.

3: Representatives and direct Taxes shall be apportioned among the several States which may be included within this Union, according to their respective Numbers, which shall be determined by adding to the whole Number of free Persons, including those bound to Service for a Term of Years, and excluding Indians not taxed, three fifths of all other Persons. The actual Enumeration shall be made within three Years after the first Meeting of the Congress of the United States, and within every subsequent Term of ten Years, in such Manner as they shall by Law direct. The Number of Representatives shall not exceed one for every thirty Thousand, but each State shall have at Least one Representative; and until such enumeration shall be made, the State of New Hampshire shall be entitled to chuse three, Massachusetts eight, Rhode-Island and Providence Plantations one, Connecticut five, New-York six, New Jersey four, Pennsylvania eight, Delaware one, Maryland six, Virginia ten, North Carolina five, South Carolina five, and Georgia three.

4: When vacancies happen in the Representation from any State, the Executive Authority thereof shall issue Writs of Election to fill such Vacancies.

5: The House of Representatives shall chuse their Speaker and other Officers; and shall have the sole Power of Impeachment.

Section 3

1: The Senate of the United States shall be composed of two Senators from each State, chosen by the Legislature thereof, for six Years; and each Senator shall have one Vote.

2: Immediately after they shall be assembled in Consequence of the first Election, they shall be divided as equally as may be into three Classes. The Seats of the Senators of the first Class shall be vacated at the Expiration of the second Year, of the second Class at the Expiration of the fourth Year, and of the third Class at the Expiration of the sixth Year, so that one third may be chosen every second Year; and if Vacancies happen by Resignation, or otherwise, during the Recess of the Legislature of any State, the Executive thereof may make temporary Appointments until the next Meeting of the Legislature, which shall then fill such Vacancies.

3: No Person shall be a Senator who shall not have attained to the Age of thirty Years, and been nine Years a Citizen of the United States, and who shall not, when elected, be an Inhabitant of that State for which he shall be chosen.

4: The Vice President of the United States shall be President of the Senate, but shall have no Vote, unless they be equally divided.

5: The Senate shall chuse their other Officers, and also a President pro tempore, in the Absence of the Vice President, or when he shall exercise the Office of President of the United States.

6: The Senate shall have the sole Power to try all Impeachments. When sitting for that Purpose, they shall be on Oath or Affirmation. When the President of the United States is tried, the Chief Justice shall preside: And no Person shall be convicted without the Concurrence of two thirds of the Members present.

7: Judgment in Cases of impeachment shall not extend further than to removal from Office, and disqualification to hold and enjoy any Office of honor, Trust or Profit under the United States: but the Party convicted shall nevertheless be liable and subject to Indictment, Trial, Judgment and Punishment, according to Law.

Section 4

1: The Times, Places and Manner of holding Elections for Senators and Representatives, shall be prescribed in each State by the Legislature thereof; but the Congress may at any time by Law make or alter such Regulations, except as to the Places of chusing Senators.

2: The Congress shall assemble at least once in every Year, and such Meeting shall be on the first Monday in December, unless they shall by Law appoint a different Day.

Section 5

1: Each House shall be the Judge of the Elections, Returns and Qualifications of its own Members, and a Majority of each shall constitute a Quorum to do Business; but a smaller Number may adjourn from day to day, and may be authorized to compel the Attendance of absent Members, in such Manner, and under such Penalties as each House may provide.

2: Each House may determine the Rules of its Proceedings, punish its Members for disorderly Behaviour, and, with the Concurrence of two thirds, expel a Member.

3: Each House shall keep a Journal of its Proceedings, and from time to time publish the same, excepting such Parts as may in their Judgment require Secrecy; and the Yeas and Nays of the Members of either House on any question shall, at the Desire of one fifth of those Present, be entered on the Journal.

4: Neither House, during the Session of Congress, shall, without the Consent of the other, adjourn for more than three days, nor to any other Place than that in which the two Houses shall be sitting.

Section 6

1: The Senators and Representatives shall receive a Compensation for their Services, to be ascertained by Law, and paid out of the Treasury of the United States. They shall in all Cases, except Treason, Felony and Breach of the Peace, be privileged from Arrest during their Attendance at the Session of their respective Houses, and in going to and returning from the same; and for any Speech or Debate in either House, they shall not be questioned in any other Place.

2: No Senator or Representative shall, during the Time for which he was elected, be appointed to any civil Office under the Authority of the United States, which shall have been created, or the Emoluments whereof shall have been encreased during such time; and no Person holding any Office under the United States, shall be a Member of either House during his Continuance in Office.

Section 7

1: All Bills for raising Revenue shall originate in the House of Representatives; but the Senate may propose or concur with Amendments as on other Bills.

2: Every Bill which shall have passed the House of Representatives and the Senate, shall, before it become a Law, be presented to the President of the United States; If he approve he shall sign it, but if not he shall return it, with his Objections to that House in which it shall have originated, who shall enter the Objections at large on their Journal, and proceed to reconsider it. If after such Reconsideration two thirds of that House shall agree to pass the Bill, it shall be sent, together with the Objections, to the other House, by which it shall likewise be reconsidered, and if approved by two thirds of that House, it shall become a Law. But in all such Cases the Votes of both Houses shall be determined by yeas and Nays, and the Names of the Persons voting for and against the Bill shall be entered on the Journal of each House respectively. If any Bill shall not be returned by the President within ten Days (Sundays excepted) after it shall have been presented to him, the Same shall be a Law, in like Manner as if he had signed it, unless the Congress by their Adjournment prevent its Return, in which Case it shall not be a Law.

3: Every Order, Resolution, or Vote to which the Concurrence of the Senate and House of Representatives may be necessary (except on a question of Adjournment) shall be presented to the President of the United States; and before the Same shall take Effect, shall be approved by him, or being disapproved by him, shall be repassed by two thirds of the Senate and House of Representatives, according to the Rules and Limitations prescribed in the Case of a Bill.

Section 8

1: The Congress shall have Power To lay and collect Taxes, Duties, Imposts and Excises, to pay the Debts and provide for the common Defence and general Welfare of the United States; but all Duties,

Imposts and Excises shall be uniform throughout the United States;

2: To borrow Money on the credit of the United States;

3: To regulate Commerce with foreign Nations, and among the several States, and with the Indian Tribes;

4: To establish an uniform Rule of Naturalization, and uniform Laws on the subject of Bankruptcies throughout the United States;

5: To coin Money, regulate the Value thereof, and of foreign Coin, and fix the Standard of Weights and Measures;

6: To provide for the Punishment of counterfeiting the Securities and current Coin of the United States;

7: To establish Post Offices and post Roads;

8: To promote the Progress of Science and useful Arts, by securing for limited Times to Authors and Inventors the exclusive Right to their respective Writings and Discoveries;

9: To constitute Tribunals inferior to the supreme Court;

10: To define and punish Piracies and Felonies committed on the high Seas, and Offences against the Law of Nations;

11: To declare War, grant Letters of Marque and Reprisal, and make Rules concerning Captures on Land and Water;

12: To raise and support Armies, but no Appropriation of Money to that Use shall be for a longer Term than two Years;

13: To provide and maintain a Navy;

14: To make Rules for the Government and Regulation of the land and naval Forces;

15: To provide for calling forth the Militia to execute the Laws of the Union, suppress Insurrections and repel Invasions;

16: To provide for organizing, arming, and disciplining, the Militia, and for governing such Part of them as may be employed in the Service of the United States, reserving to the States respectively, the Appointment of the Officers, and the Authority of training the Militia according to the discipline prescribed by Congress;

17: To exercise exclusive Legislation in all Cases whatsoever, over such District (not exceeding ten Miles square) as may, by Cession of particular States, and the Acceptance of Congress, become the Seat of the Government of the United States, and to exercise like Authority over all Places purchased by the Consent of the Legislature of the State in which the Same shall be, for the Erection of Forts, Magazines, Arsenals, dock-Yards, and other needful Buildings;—And

18: To make all Laws which shall be necessary and proper for carrying into Execution the foregoing Powers, and all other Powers vested by this Constitution in the Government of the United States, or in any Department or Officer thereof.

Section 9

1: The Migration or Importation of such Persons as any of the States now existing shall think proper to admit, shall not be prohibited by the Congress prior to the Year one thousand eight hundred and eight, but a Tax or duty may be imposed on such Importation, not exceeding ten dollars for each Person.

2: The Privilege of the Writ of Habeas Corpus shall not be suspended, unless when in Cases of Rebellion or Invasion the public Safety may require it.

3: No Bill of Attainder or ex post facto Law shall be passed.

4: No Capitation, or other direct, Tax shall be laid, unless in Proportion to the Census or Enumeration herein before directed to be taken.

5: No Tax or Duty shall be laid on Articles exported from any State.

6: No Preference shall be given by any Regulation of Commerce or Revenue to the Ports of one State over those of another: nor shall Vessels bound to, or from, one State, be obliged to enter, clear, or pay Duties in another.

7: No Money shall be drawn from the Treasury, but in Consequence of Appropriations made by Law; and a regular Statement and Account of the Receipts and Expenditures of all public Money shall be published from time to time.

8: No Title of Nobility shall be granted by the United States: And no Person holding any Office of Profit or Trust under them, shall, without the Consent of the Congress, accept of any present, Emolument, Office, or Title, of any kind whatever, from any King, Prince, or foreign State.

Section 10

1: No State shall enter into any Treaty, Alliance, or Confederation; grant Letters of Marque and Reprisal; coin Money; emit Bills of Credit; make any Thing but gold and silver Coin a Tender in Payment of Debts; pass any Bill of Attainder, ex post facto Law, or Law impairing the Obligation of Contracts, or grant any Title of Nobility.

2: No State shall, without the Consent of the Congress, lay any Imposts or Duties on Imports or Exports, except what may be absolutely necessary for executing it's inspection Laws: and the net Produce of all Duties and Imposts, laid by any State on Imports or Exports, shall be for the Use of the Treasury of the United States; and all such Laws shall be subject to the Revision and Controul of the Congress.

3: No State shall, without the Consent of Congress, lay any Duty of Tonnage, keep Troops, or Ships of War in time of Peace, enter into any Agreement or Compact with another State, or with a foreign Power, or engage in War, unless actually invaded, or in such imminent Danger as will not admit of delay.

Article II (Article 2 - Executive)

Section 1

1: The executive Power shall be vested in a President of the United States of America. He shall hold his Office during the Term of four Years, and, together with the Vice President, chosen for the same Term, be elected, as follows

2: Each State shall appoint, in such Manner as the Legislature thereof may direct, a Number of Electors, equal to the whole Number of Senators and Representatives to which the State may be entitled in the Congress: but no Senator or Representative, or Person holding an Office of Trust or Profit under the United States, shall be appointed an Elector.

3: The Electors shall meet in their respective States, and vote by Ballot for two Persons, of whom one at least shall not be an Inhabitant of the same State with themselves. And they shall make a List of all the Persons voted for, and of the Number of Votes for each; which List they shall sign and certify, and transmit sealed to the Seat of the Government of the United States, directed to the President of the Senate. The President of the Senate shall, in the Presence of the Senate and House of

Representatives, open all the Certificates, and the Votes shall then be counted. The Person having the greatest Number of Votes shall be the President, if such Number be a Majority of the whole Number of Electors appointed; and if there be more than one who have such Majority, and have an equal Number of Votes, then the House of Representatives shall immediately chuse by Ballot one of them for President; and if no Person have a Majority, then from the five highest on the List the said House shall in like Manner chuse the President. But in chusing the President, the Votes shall be taken by States, the Representation from each State having one Vote; A quorum for this Purpose shall consist of a Member or Members from two thirds of the States, and a Majority of all the States shall be necessary to a Choice. In every Case, after the Choice of the President, the Person having the greatest Number of Votes of the Electors shall be the Vice President. But if there should remain two or more who have equal Votes, the Senate shall chuse from them by Ballot the Vice President.

4: The Congress may determine the Time of chusing the Electors, and the Day on which they shall give their Votes; which Day shall be the same throughout the United States.

5: No Person except a natural born Citizen, or a Citizen of the United States, at the time of the Adoption of this Constitution, shall be eligible to the Office of President; neither shall any Person be eligible to that Office who shall not have attained to the Age of thirty five Years, and been fourteen Years a Resident within the United States.

6: In Case of the Removal of the President from Office, or of his Death, Resignation, or Inability to discharge the Powers and Duties of the said Office, the Same shall devolve on the Vice President, and the Congress may by Law provide for the Case of Removal, Death, Resignation or Inability, both of the President and Vice President, declaring what Officer shall then act as President, and such Officer shall act accordingly, until the Disability be removed, or a President shall be elected.

7: The President shall, at stated Times, receive for his Services, a Compensation, which shall neither be encreased nor diminished during the Period for which he shall have been elected, and he shall not receive within that Period any other Emolument from the United States, or any of them.

8: Before he enter on the Execution of his Office, he shall take the following Oath or Affirmation:—"I do solemnly swear (or affirm) that I will faithfully execute the Office of President of the United States, and will to the best of my Ability, preserve, protect and defend the Constitution of the United States."

Section 2

1: The President shall be Commander in Chief of the Army and Navy of the United States, and of the Militia of the several States, when called into the actual Service of the United States; he may require the Opinion, in writing, of the principal Officer in each of the executive Departments, upon any Subject relating to the Duties of their respective Offices, and he shall have Power to grant Reprieves and Pardons for Offences against the United States, except in Cases of Impeachment.

2: He shall have Power, by and with the Advice and Consent of the Senate, to make Treaties, provided two thirds of the Senators present concur; and he shall nominate, and by and with the Advice and Consent of the Senate, shall appoint Ambassadors, other public Ministers and Consuls, Judges of the supreme Court, and all other Officers of the United States, whose Appointments are not herein otherwise provided for, and which shall be established by Law: but the Congress may by Law vest the Appointment of such inferior Officers, as they think proper, in the President alone, in the Courts of Law, or in the Heads of Departments.

3: The President shall have Power to fill up all Vacancies that may happen during the Recess of the Senate, by granting Commissions which shall expire at the End of their next Session.

Section 3

He shall from time to time give to the Congress Information of the State of the Union, and recommend to their Consideration such Measures as he shall judge necessary and expedient; he may, on extraordinary Occasions, convene both Houses, or either of them, and in Case of Disagreement between them, with Respect to the Time of Adjournment, he may adjourn them to such Time as he shall think proper; he shall receive Ambassadors and other public Ministers; he shall take Care that the Laws be faithfully executed, and shall Commission all the Officers of the United States.

Section 4

The President, Vice President and all civil Officers of the United States, shall be removed from Office on Impeachment for, and Conviction of, Treason, Bribery, or other high Crimes and Misdemeanors.

Article III (Article 3 - Judicial)

Section 1

The judicial Power of the United States, shall be vested in one supreme Court, and in such inferior Courts as the Congress may from time to time ordain and establish. The Judges, both of the supreme and inferior Courts, shall hold their Offices during good Behaviour, and shall, at stated Times, receive for their Services, a Compensation, which shall not be diminished during their Continuance in Office.

Section 2

1: The judicial Power shall extend to all Cases, in Law and Equity, arising under this Constitution, the Laws of the United States, and Treaties made, or which shall be made, under their Authority;—to all Cases affecting Ambassadors, other public Ministers and Consuls;—to all Cases of admiralty and maritime Jurisdiction;—to Controversies to which the United States shall be a Party;—to

Controversies between two or more States;—between a State and Citizens of another State; — between Citizens of different States, —between Citizens of the same State claiming Lands under Grants of different States, and between a State, or the Citizens thereof, and foreign States, Citizens or Subjects.

2: In all Cases affecting Ambassadors, other public Ministers and Consuls, and those in which a State shall be Party, the supreme Court shall have original Jurisdiction. In all the other Cases before mentioned, the supreme Court shall have appellate Jurisdiction, both as to Law and Fact, with such Exceptions, and under such Regulations as the Congress shall make.

3: The Trial of all Crimes, except in Cases of Impeachment, shall be by Jury; and such Trial shall be held in the State where the said Crimes shall have been committed; but when not committed within any State, the Trial shall be at such Place or Places as the Congress may by Law have directed.

Section 3

1: Treason against the United States, shall consist only in levying War against them, or in adhering to their Enemies, giving them Aid and Comfort. No Person shall be convicted of Treason unless on the Testimony of two Witnesses to the same overt Act, or on Confession in open Court.

2: The Congress shall have Power to declare the Punishment of Treason, but no Attainder of Treason shall work Corruption of Blood, or Forfeiture except during the Life of the Person attainted.

Article IV (Article 4 - States' Relations)

Section 1

Full Faith and Credit shall be given in each State to the public Acts, Records, and judicial Proceedings of every other State. And the Congress may by general Laws prescribe the Manner in which such

Acts, Records and Proceedings shall be proved, and the Effect thereof.

Section 2

1: The Citizens of each State shall be entitled to all Privileges and Immunities of Citizens in the several States.

2: A Person charged in any State with Treason, Felony, or other Crime, who shall flee from Justice, and be found in another State, shall on Demand of the executive Authority of the State from which he fled, be delivered up, to be removed to the State having Jurisdiction of the Crime.

3: No Person held to Service or Labour in one State, under the Laws thereof, escaping into another, shall, in Consequence of any Law or Regulation therein, be discharged from such Service or Labour, but shall be delivered up on Claim of the Party to whom such Service or Labour may be due.

Section 3

1: New States may be admitted by the Congress into this Union; but no new State shall be formed or erected within the Jurisdiction of any other State; nor any State be formed by the Junction of two or more States, or Parts of States, without the Consent of the Legislatures of the States concerned as well as of the Congress.

2: The Congress shall have Power to dispose of and make all needful Rules and Regulations respecting the Territory or other Property belonging to the United States; and nothing in this Constitution shall be so construed as to Prejudice any Claims of the United States, or of any particular State.

Section 4

The United States shall guarantee to every State in this Union a Republican Form of Government, and shall protect each of them against Invasion; and on Application of the Legislature, or of the Executive (when the Legislature cannot be convened) against domestic Violence.

Article V (Article 5 - Mode of Amendment)

The Congress, whenever two thirds of both Houses shall deem it necessary, shall propose Amendments to this Constitution, or, on the Application of the Legislatures of two thirds of the several States, shall call a Convention for proposing Amendments, which, in either Case, shall be valid to all Intents and Purposes, as Part of this Constitution, when ratified by the Legislatures of three fourths of the several States, or by Conventions in three fourths thereof, as the one or the other Mode of Ratification may be proposed by the Congress; Provided that no Amendment which may be made prior to the Year One thousand eight hundred and eight shall in any Manner affect the first and fourth Clauses in the Ninth Section of the first Article; and that no State, without its Consent, shall be deprived of its equal Suffrage in the Senate.

Article VI (Article 6 - Prior Debts, National Supremacy, Oaths of Office)

1: All Debts contracted and Engagements entered into, before the Adoption of this Constitution, shall be as valid against the United States under this Constitution, as under the Confederation.

2: This Constitution, and the Laws of the United States which shall be made in Pursuance thereof; and all Treaties made, or which shall be made, under the Authority of the United States, shall be the supreme Law of the Land; and the Judges in every State shall be bound thereby, any Thing in the Constitution or Laws of any State to the Contrary notwithstanding.

3: The Senators and Representatives before mentioned, and the Members of the several State Legislatures, and all executive and judicial Officers, both of the United States and of the several States, shall be bound by Oath or Affirmation, to support this Constitution; but no religious Test shall ever be required as a Qualification to any Office or public Trust under the United States.

Article VII (Article 7 - Ratification)

The Ratification of the Conventions of nine States, shall be sufficient for the Establishment of this Constitution between the States so ratifying the Same.

BILL OF RIGHTS

The ten amendments that comprise the Bill of Rights are as follows:

Preamble to the Bill of Rights

*Congress of the United States

begun and held at the City of New-York, on Wednesday the fourth of March one thousand seven hundred and eighty-nine.

THE Conventions of a number of the States, having at the time of their adopting the Constitution, expressed a desire, in order to prevent misconstruction or abuse of its powers, that further declaratory and restrictive clauses should be added: And as extending the ground of public confidence in the Government, will best ensure the beneficent ends of its institution. RESOLVED by the Senate and House of Representatives of the United States of America, in Congress assembled, two thirds of both Houses concurring, that the following Articles be proposed to the Legislatures of the several States, as amendments to the Constitution of the United States, all, or any of which Articles, when ratified by three fourths of the said Legislatures, to be valid to all intents and purposes, as part of the said Constitution; viz. ARTICLES in addition to, and Amendment of the Constitution of the United States of America, proposed by Congress, and ratified by the Legislatures of the several States, pursuant to the fifth Article of the original Constitution.

Frederick Augustus Muhlenberg Speaker of the House of Representatives John Adams, Vice-President of the United States and President of the Senate.

Attest, John Beckley, Clerk of the House of Representatives. Sam. A. Otis Secretary of the Senate. *On September 25, 1789, Congress transmitted to the state legislatures twelve proposed amendments, two of which, having to do with Congressional representation and Congressional pay, were not adopted. The remaining ten amendments became the Bill of Rights.

Amendment 1

- Freedom of Religion, Speech, and the Press

Congress shall make no law respecting an establishment of religion or prohibiting the free exercise thereof or abridging the freedom of speech or of the press, or the right of the people peaceably to assemble and to petition the government for a redress of grievances.

Amendment 2

- The Right to Bear Arms

A well-regulated Militia being necessary to the security of a free State, the right of the people to keep and bear Arms shall not be infringed.

Amendment 3

- The Housing of Soldiers

No soldier shall, in time of peace, be quartered in any house without the consent of the owner, nor in time of war but in a manner to be prescribed by law.

Amendment 4

- Protection from Unreasonable Searches and Seizures

The right of the people to be secure in their persons, houses, papers, and effects against unreasonable searches and seizures shall not be violated, and no warrants shall issue but upon probable cause, supported by oath or affirmation, and particularly describing the place to be searched and the persons or things to be seized.

Amendment 5

- Protection of Rights to Life, Liberty, and Property

No person shall be held to answer for a capital or otherwise infamous crime unless on a presentment or indictment of a grand jury, except in cases arising in the land or naval forces, or in the militia, when in actual service in time of war or public danger; nor shall any person be subject for the same offense to be twice put in jeopardy of life or limb; nor shall be compelled in any criminal case to be a witness against himself, nor be deprived of life, liberty, or property without due process of law; nor shall private property be taken for public use without just compensation.

Amendment 6

- Rights of Accused Persons in Criminal Cases

In all criminal prosecutions, the accused shall enjoy the right to a speedy and public trial by an impartial jury of the state and district wherein the crime shall have been committed, which district shall have been previously ascertained by law, and to be informed of the nature and cause of the accusation; to be confronted with the witnesses against him; to have compulsory process for obtaining witnesses in his favor; and to have the assistance of counsel for his defense.

Amendment 7

- Rights in Civil Cases

In suits at common law, where the value in controversy shall exceed twenty dollars, the right of trial by jury shall be preserved, and no fact tried by a jury shall be otherwise reexamined in any court of the United States than according to the rules of the common law.

Amendment 8

- Excessive Bail, Fines, and Punishments Forbidden

Excessive bail shall not be required, nor excessive fines imposed, nor cruel and unusual punishments inflicted.

Amendment 9

- Other Rights Kept by the People

The enumeration in the Constitution of certain rights shall not be construed to deny or disparage others retained by the people.

Amendment 10

- Undelegated Powers Kept by the States and the People

The powers not delegated to the United States by the Constitution, nor prohibited by it to the states, are reserved to the states respectively, or to the people.

BIBLIOGRAPHY

Barnett, Randy E., Second Edition, "The Structure of Liberty, Justice & the Rule of Law" Oxford, United Kingdom, Oxford University Press, 2014

Barnett, Randy E., Updated Edition, "Restoring the Lost Constitution, The Presumption of Liberty" Princeton, New Jersey, Princeton University Press 2014

Bloom, Allan, Editor, "Confronting the Constitution" Washington D.C., The AEI Press, 1987

Donnelly, Jack, Third Edition, "Universal Human Rights in Theory and Practice" Ithica, New York, Cornell University Press, 2013

Ferguson, Robert A., Introduction and Notes, "The Federalist, Alexander Hamilton, James Madison, and John Jay" New York, Barnes and Nobel Classics 2006

Harrison, T. R., "Hobbes, Locke, and Confusion's Masterpiece" Cambridge, United Kingdom, Cambridge University Press, 2003

Hobbes, Thomas, "Leviathan" Digireads.com Publishing 2017

Locke, John, "Two Treatises of Government" London, United Kingdom, Tuttle Publishing 1993

Rousseau, Jean-Jacques, translated and edited by John T. Scott, "The Major Political Writings of Jean-Jacques Rosseau" Chicago, Illinois, University of Chicago Press, 2014

Swanson, Mary-Elaine, "John Locke, Philosopher of American History" Ventura, California, Nordskog Publishing, 2013

West, Thomas G., "The Political Theory of the American Founding, Natural Rights, Public Policy, and The Moral Conditions of Freedom" Cambridge, United Kingdom, Cambridge University Press, 2017

ABOUT THE AUTHOR

Don Jans has studied history from a very early age. He gravitated toward Russian history and from there found his way to Karl Marx and the study of Marxism. The more he understood the philosophy of Marx, the clearer it became that what was being touted as the American way by many in the United States was in fact the way to an American collectivist society.

Don has written three other books on the topic of Marxism and how it is permeating and fundamentally transforming the United States.

MY GRANDCHILDRENS AMERICA

GOODBYE CONSTITUTION, FREEDOM, AMERICA

THE ROAD TO TYRANNY

The books are available on Amazon, Branes & Nobel and at www.mygrandchildrensamerica.com

Don has spoken to many different groups around the United States and can be contacted at

mygrandchildrensamerica@gmail.com